Greenhouse Plants

Created and designed by
the editorial staff of
ORTHO BOOKS

Project Editor
Elaine Ratner

Writer
James L. Jones

Photographer
Tovah Martin

Designer
Gary Hespenheide

Ortho Books

Publisher
Edward A. Evans

Editorial Director
Christine Jordan

Production Director
Ernie S. Tasaki

Managing Editors
Michael D. Smith
Sally W. Smith

System Manager
Linda M. Bouchard

National Sales Manager
J. D. Gillis

**National Accounts Manager—
 Book Trade**
Paul D. Wiedemann

Marketing Specialist
Dennis M. Castle

Distribution Specialist
Barbara F. Steadham

Operations Assistant
Georgiann Wright

Administrative Assistant
Francine Lorentz-Olson

Technical Consultant
J. A. Crozier, Jr., Ph.D.

Address all inquiries to
Ortho Books
Chevron Chemical Company
Consumer Products Division
Box 5047
San Ramon, CA 94583

Chevron Chemical Company
6001 Bollinger Canyon Road, San Ramon, CA 94583

Acknowledgments

Photo Editor
Dick Schuettge

Consultant
Dr. Robert Ornduff,
 Department of Botany, University of
 California, Berkeley

Copy Chief
Melinda E. Levine

Editorial Coordinator
Cass Dempsey

Copyeditor
Andrew Alden

Proofreader
Deborah Bruner

Indexer
Frances Bowles

Editorial Assistant
John Parr

Layout by
Cindy Putnam

Composition by
Nancy P. McCune
Laurie A. Steele

Production by
Studio 165

Separations by
Color Tech Corporation

Lithographed in the USA by
Webcrafters, Inc.

Special Thanks to
Larry Hodgson, Sillery, Quebec
Pamela and Jim Leaver, San Miguel Greenhouse,
 Concord, Calif.
Rod McClellan Co., South San Francisco, Calif.
Elvin McDonald, Brooklyn Botanical Gardens,
 Brooklyn, N.Y.
Larry Moskovitz, Orchidanica, Oakland, Calif.
Mary Sullivan
Debbie, Becky, Ben, and Tracey

Additional Photographers
With the exception of the following, all photographs in this book are by Tovah Martin at Logee's Greenhouses, Danielson, Conn. Names of photographers are followed by the page numbers on which their work appears. R = right, C = center, L = left, T = top, B = bottom.

William C. Aplin: 59
M. Baker: 39
Laurie A. Black: 15, 17T, 40
John Blaustein: 28
Alan Copeland: 7T, 18
D. Hatch: 32
Saxon Holt: 20, 37
James L. Jones: 17B, 50L, 58L, 60R, 61TR, 70, 103L
Charles Kennard: 10
R. Kriner: 31
Michael Landis: 26, 35, 58R
R. E. Lyons: 29
Michael McKinley: 56T, 57L
Picnic Productions: 56BL
Pam Peirce: 46
Karen Stafford Rantzman: Front cover, title page, 4, 8, 12, 24, 27, 42, 53, 89BL
Ron West: 30, 33TR, BR

Front Cover
Aechmea fasciata, center, surrounded by, clockwise from top left, *Hibiscus rosa-sinensis*, *Adiantum hispidulum*, *Vriesia* species, and two *Begonia rex* cultivars.

Back Cover
Top left: *Vallota speciosa*

Top right: *Punica granatum* 'Wonderful'

Bottom left: *Coleus thrysoides*

Bottom right: *Strelitzia regina*

Title Page
Bromeliads are striking greenhouse plants with distinctive foliage and, sometimes, lovely flowers. Top to bottom: *Aechmea fasciata*, *Guzmania* hybrids, *Aechmea luddemanniana*.

PLANTS IN THE GREENHOUSE

In the protected environment of a greenhouse, the weather is always right for gardening. Flowers bloom all winter, and plants that often struggle to survive outside grow easily to their full potential.

Greenhouse Plants

CARING FOR GREENHOUSE PLANTS

A wide variety of plants will thrive in the warm, sunny atmosphere of a greenhouse, asking only an appropriate growing medium and a standard program of watering, feeding, and pest control.

PLANT DIRECTORY

All the plants in the alphabetical directory have something special to contribute to a home greenhouse. Many bear colorful flowers in winter. Some provide fruit, or herbs, or fragrance to perfume the air. The range of color, size, shape, and habit is vast; the choice is yours.

Plants in the Greenhouse

In the protected environment of a greenhouse, the weather is always right for gardening. Flowers bloom all winter, and plants that often struggle to survive outside grow easily to their full potential.

There are few havens more pleasant than the interior of a greenhouse on a winter day. It is warm, still, and humid and above all, it is filled with the sight and aroma of growing plants. But which plants? Which species do well in such an environment, and which are worth the effort and space devoted to growing them? How does a greenhouse gardener choose from the large range of possibilities?

The purpose of this book is to help you to choose and successfully grow the best plants for your particular greenhouse. The first chapter discusses the basic criteria for selection: the kind of greenhouse you have, your personal goals as a gardener, and the needs and potential benefits of various types of plants.

The next chapter examines the day-to-day care of greenhouse plants, from watering and fertilizing to pest control and propagation.

The remainder and by far the greatest portion of the book is an illustrated "Plant Directory." In it you will find hundreds of plants that thrive in the greenhouse environment.

A greenhouse is a three-dimensional equivalent of an artist's empty canvas, waiting to be filled with living color and form. Here ferns and other foliage plants are set beneath and behind a spectacular arrangement featuring orchids and bromeliads.

CHOOSING GREENHOUSE PLANTS

There are two main considerations in choosing: the appeal of a plant to the gardener, and its suitability for the greenhouse. The matter of appeal naturally comes first. Is the species ornamental enough in form, foliage, and flower to merit a place in the greenhouse? Do the flowers come at the time of year when they're most needed and appreciated, such as those of *Camellia sasanqua* in November and *Daphne odora* in February? Does the plant have a little something extra—edible fruit perhaps, or fragrant foliage (*Helichrysum* species), or flowers (*Daphne* species, again), or clippings for the stew pot?

These characteristics are among the common elements of appeal. The alphabetical "Plant Directory" that begins on page 43 indicates how readily some or all of them can be achieved. All of the plants described in this book are ornamental, most of them all of the time, although some have brief periods of browning leaves before dormancy.

Useful Plants

Among the listed species that are useful as well as ornamental are fruit-bearers such as *Citrus, Eriobotrya, Eugenia, Feijoa, Fortunella, Malpighia, Passiflora, Psidium,* and *Syzygium,* and herbs such as *Eucalyptus, Pelargonium,* and *Rosmarinus.* They are included because in addition to being useful, they are suitable to a greenhouse. Other useful but unsuitable plants, such as the tomato, *Lycopersicon,* are not included. Although the tomato is a feasible greenhouse plant, widely grown in commercial greenhouses, it is hardly ornamental and needs a great deal of light, room, warmth, support, and protection from pests. In any case, tomatoes are always available at the supermarket and can be easily grown outside during the summer. The fruit-bearing plants described in this book may have one or another of these shortcomings, but not so many wrapped up in a single species.

Season, Size, and Suitability

The plants in this book, in addition to being ornamental, are chosen for their season of bloom (with preference given to fall and winter), appropriate size, and special suitability for the greenhouse. The appeal of fall and

winter flowers speaks for itself. Appropriate size is not as clear-cut. The optimum species would remain pot-sized forever, but many growers wouldn't dream of being without *Camellia* species, for instance, even though it will tend to outgrow pot and greenhouse in time. Drastic pruning may be the answer, or simply accepting that not all species need to be permanent.

Special suitability also needs some explanation. There are many fine groups of plants that are not included in this book or that are treated more summarily than their popularity would suggest. These are plants that can be grown more satisfactorily in the house itself, are primarily grown for foliage, or belong to a group so filled with suitable species that it

One of the greatest attractions of greenhouse gardening is having an array of beautiful flowers throughout the winter. The long-lasting blooms of the moth orchid, Phalaenopsis, *bring cheer all winter to a heated greenhouse. (It does not thrive below 65° F.)*

Left: Many greenhouse plants are available at florist shops or local commercial greenhouses. Bottom: Many more are available by mail. Mail-order greenhouses are expert at packing plants; they arrive in fine condition, ready for planting.

merits a book of its own (such groups are mentioned, but not described in lengthy detail). In addition, plants that are too large, too unwieldy, or, in some cases, too smelly for the greenhouse have been omitted.

Where to Buy

All of the plants described are available to home greenhouse gardeners. Some, the most familiar, can be found at most florists' shops or at least at a local commercial greenhouse. Begonias, bromeliads, cacti, and other succulents will always be on hand there. Genera that are quite familiar but are considered greenhouse rather than house plants, such as *Citrus, Camellia,* and *Rosmarinus,* will be found in a smaller number of more diversified commercial greenhouses, usually located in or near a good-sized city. They are readily available to people who live within driving distance of such a city, but not to many others. However, those plants and many that are more exotic can be acquired by anyone in the country from mail-order suppliers (see "Mail-Order Sources," page 108).

Each mail-order supplier has its own specialty. Packaging and delivery are in most cases so good that the plants suffer no serious setback and arrive almost as ready to go as those brought home from the florist.

Finally, there are the seed companies, both domestic and foreign (see page 108). Some plants, such as *Eucalyptus* species, are best

propagated by seed. Others, such as *Protea*, are so exotic and specialized that few nurseries stock them, so seed companies are really the only source.

Practically speaking, each genus described, even *Eucalyptus*, has some species that are available as mail-order plants. A readiness to order plants through the mail is therefore a valuable tool in achieving a distinctive, diversified greenhouse garden.

When all is said and done, the suitability of any plant depends on the nature of its surroundings. The success of any individual species will be determined by how fully its needs are met by the characteristics of its greenhouse environment.

THE GREENHOUSE ENVIRONMENT

The term *greenhouse* can be applied to any structure that traps and stores solar energy by means of transparent panels. A sunporch, sunroom, or even a sunny window can provide

some of the benefits of a greenhouse. In common parlance, however, a greenhouse is a structure specifically designed to have as much transparent surface as possible oriented toward the sun. That is the type of structure referred to as a greenhouse in this book. Bear in mind that this definition does not specify the method of heating; a greenhouse can be heated by the sun alone (solar greenhouse or sunhouse) or it can be warmed by supplemental heat provided by fossil fuels, electricity, or other means.

Why a Greenhouse?

The outdoors in any given location offers a particular range of environments, some sunny, some sheltered from the wind, some shadier, or breezier, or more exposed. A greenhouse adds a whole new range. The indoor greenhouse environment, although not necessarily better, is different in quite fundamental ways. That difference not only broadens the possible choice of plants—although that in itself is a dazzling revelation—it also makes new styles of gardening possible.

The garden environment in a greenhouse is defined, confined, isolated, and comfortable. It is *defined* in size, shape, and climate, each of which can be controlled by the gardener and which together define the type of garden that can exist inside. It is *confined* by the walls and glazing, which put strict limits on the size of plants and on the extent of weeding. It is *isolated* from the outdoors, holding in stillness and warmth on the one hand, while on the other shutting out rain and the local predators that would make short work of greenhouse pests. It is *comfortable,* always. Wind and cold do not intrude; snow does not hide the plants from view. In a greenhouse it is always summer or at least spring, and there are no mosquitoes.

It is true that the weather is milder the year around in some parts of the country, but even in these areas, a greenhouse can be a valuable adjunct to gardening. It provides the extra bit of warmth that truly tropical plants may require. It offers protection from wind and rain and allows the gardener to control humidity in arid regions. A greenhouse in a winter-rainfall region will keep succulents such as cacti from excessive winter moisture. Heating requirements are minimal in mild climates, and very likely can be met by solar heating alone.

Gardeners with a greenhouse can grow plants they have read about but never seen— *Cantua, Correa,* flowering *Eucalyptus,* beautiful blue *Tibouchina,* and the most dazzling of all, *Protea.* They can grow the familiar favorites—begonias, bromeliads, citrus, gesneriads, primulas, pelargoniums, succulents—in the grandest style. And they can enjoy bloom in winter, when *Babiana, Camellia, Cyclamen, Daphne, Jasminum, Narcissus,* and others are at their best.

Plant Origins

Where do greenhouse plants come from originally, that they are so well suited to this particular environment? There is no single, tidy answer. In fact, greenhouse conditions are so fundamentally beneficial to plants, there are very few species that won't profit from them. Still, greenhouse plants tend to fall into several broad categories.

Rainforest A warm, humid, and unchanging environment, dim on the ground and bright in the canopy. The rainforest is home to orchids and bromeliads in the treetops, aroids (such as *Philodendron*) in the depths, and

Loved for their delicate flowers are Oncidium, *top, and* Scutellaria javanica, *bottom.*

All plants adapt to their natural environments; when those environments are approximated within a greenhouse, the plants are very much at home. Desert plants are used to broad temperature swings and so do well in unheated greenhouses, where the heat of the sun provides warmth by day and the temperature falls considerably at night.

begonias at many points in between. The forest floor species tend to be better houseplants than greenhouse plants. This may be surprising given the stark difference in humidity between habitat and home, but in fact a number of houseplants such as philodendron are semi-epiphytic; they have water-conserving leaves to cope with periods of moisture deprivation at their roots. Many other forest-floor houseplants, used to contending with seasons of little or no rain, also have water-conserving leaves.

Desert   An arid, very bright environment, with extreme ranges of heat and cold. Cacti and other succulents that flourish here can be either very difficult or very easy to cultivate, depending on whether or not they have specialized in a hard-to-duplicate niche. In general, desert plants are well suited to the wide temperature swings characteristic of a solar greenhouse.

Warm-temperate regions   Just like home only warmer, with a touch or more of cold and snow. This is a rich source of many excellent and adaptable greenhouse plants, including winter bloomers. The Mediterranean is a particularly generous region, providing many tough, hardy, attractive plants of an appropriate size, such as *Convolvulus cneorum, Erodium chamaedryoides, Helichrysum angustifolium,* and *Narcissus bulbocodium.*

Surprisingly, parts of Australia can also be considered warm-temperate in that species there have an unexpected and currently unnecessary hardiness (not long ago, in millions of years, Australia was much farther from the equator than it is now). Many *Eucalyptus* species can stand a little to a lot of frost; some of the tea-trees (*Leptospermum*) can go down to 12° F.

Parts of South America (the source of *Fuchsia* and *Passiflora*) and most of China

(the source of *Camellia, Citrus,* and *Daphne odora*) are warm-temperate. South Africa varies between temperate and tropical for groups of plants that grow side by side; *Protea* species have very little hardiness, but *Nerine bowdenii* can withstand temperatures to 12° F.

Inside the Greenhouse

A greenhouse is widely receptive to a broad range of plants, mostly because of the brightness, warmth, and humidity it offers.

Brightness A greenhouse is effectively as bright as the same space would be if unenclosed. There is actually some light reduction, since glass and plastic transmit only about 90 percent of the incident light, but this slight decrease has no effect on the growth rate of the plants.

The majority of plants are reasonably flexible in their requirements for light. Three or four hours of sun per day in the growing season, direct or lightly shaded, is sufficient for good health, compact growth, and ample flowering. When not in growth, which is wintertime for most plants, much less light is needed, particularly under cool conditions.

There are important groups, however, such as *Cyclamen* species, that are dormant in summer and active in winter. They tend to be satisfied with the weak winter sunlight, but should get as much as possible. It is not a problem if the greenhouse is at times so blanketed with snow that the interior is quite dim, so long as it doesn't happen too often or last too long.

Warmth The greenhouse effect works in two ways to raise the interior temperature of an enclosed structure with a transparent covering exposed to the sun. First, light is admitted. A portion is promptly reflected back out of the greenhouse by surfaces inside, and another portion is absorbed. The object that does the absorbing, be it plant, pot, brick, or dirt, is warmed. It then reradiates some of the energy absorbed at a longer wavelength, as infrared or heat radiation. The glazing of the greenhouse is opaque to the longer wavelength, and so that energy cannot escape. Second, heated air inside the greenhouse is prevented from mixing with the outside atmosphere. The degree and duration of warming depends on the

design, construction, and location of the greenhouse and the presence of objects inside that can absorb and store the sun's heat, but any greenhouse structure has a minimum temperature higher than that outside.

The warmth within a greenhouse benefits the garden in several ways. First, the minimum temperature of air and soil is increased. In general, each step upward in minimum temperature opens up more plant possibilities than it closes off; a warmer greenhouse can shelter a wider range of species than a cooler greenhouse. Take the genus *Camellia* as an example. One species, *C. japonica,* can be grown in a cold (4° F) greenhouse. Two species, *C. japonica* and *C. sasanqua,* can be grown in a somewhat warmer (12° F) greenhouse, and five species—those two plus *C. chrysantha, C. lutchuensis,* and *C. reticulata*—can be grown in one that remains above freezing.

It is worth asking how much has been gained by warming the greenhouse. To continue our example, *Camellia sasanqua* and *C. japonica* provide their respective fall and winter blooms in greenhouses with both above- and below-freezing temperatures. The fragrance of *C. lutchuensis* is not possible in a below-freezing greenhouse, but it can be compensated for by

Camellia sasanqua *is one of many plants that bloom in winter as long as the temperature in the greenhouse does not go too low—in this case as long as it stays above 28° F.*

Helichrysum psilolepis *hangs high up in a greenhouse. Hanging baskets add visual interest, and make it possible to grow more plants with less crowding.*

Daphne odora. Camellia chrysantha and *C. reticulata* are rather too large and rangy for the greenhouse in any case. Nonetheless, if you wish to grow the more tender species, raising the minimum temperature can be well worth the extra effort required.

Another benefit of a warmer greenhouse is that it both extends the growing season and increases the temperature during the season. The result is more rapid plant development and, in particular, less time required for plants to reach flowering size.

Note, however, that the higher the temperature the more active the insects and mites, and the lower the humidity.

In a closed-in greenhouse there is no clear-cut upper limit to the temperature. Long before uncomfortably high temperatures are reached, however, the gardener is going to introduce some form of ventilation to keep the interior tolerable for plants and people. In fact, ventilation, getting rid of heat, is at least as important as heating.

Most species, certainly those generally considered to be greenhouse plants, thrive in temperatures from 70° F up when in active growth. The upper limit of their tolerance is actually set more by lowered humidity than by elevated temperature and varies from species to species. *Eucalyptus macrocarpa* and *Protea cynaroides*, for instance, are unaffected when the

Opposite: If plants share approximately the same needs for warmth and humidity, they should grow well together. Mixing plants of different colors and habits of growth can produce striking displays.

temperature inside approaches 100° F, but *Primula obconica* wilts and is overrun by spider mites at temperatures well below that.

Within the comfort range, vegetative growth may be spurred at higher temperatures, but the flowering cycle is likely to be foreshortened. That is to say, blooms last longer and remain in better shape when conditions are cooler. This can be a major consideration in a greenhouse garden.

Another factor that may enter in is that some species require cool, even cold temperatures to set buds. For this reason *Daphne odora* and *Rosmarinus officinalis* are more floriferous in a below-freezing greenhouse though they will grow perfectly well in a warmer one.

Many winter-blooming bulbous genera that are dormant in summer, such as *Babiana, Haemanthus*, and *Ixia*, need hot, dry summer conditions to prepare for the next winter's growth and flowering.

Humidity   For the majority of ornamental plants, the higher the humidity, up to a limit, the better the performance. In a typical home in winter, if the temperature is set at about 65° F the relative humidity is about 30 percent. In a cool greenhouse, the humidity is at or above 70 percent. This makes all the difference to a plant. Transpiration, the transport of water through the plant from roots to leaves, from where it is evaporated into the air, is slowed; slower transpiration reduces the likelihood of drought stress at the roots and leaves. Reduced stress, in turn, means a stronger plant, and greater strength means greater resistance to pests and disease. Remember, however, that the relative humidity is dependent on the temperature of the greenhouse, and humidity will fall too low for many plants in a strongly heated greenhouse unless steps are taken to introduce more moisture into the air.

Excessive humidity, 90 percent or above, will cause mildewed leaves and rotted stems and roots in certain species, including most of the succulents. Such a high humidity level is not likely to occur in a properly constructed and operated greenhouse, but may be brought on by poor drainage, excessive watering, or insufficient air exchange. The last can be a problem in a very tight greenhouse, such as one shrouded in polyethylene for the winter.

It is important to pay careful attention to temperature and humidity. Too much heat or not enough, too much or too little moisture can cause stress to plants and keep them from blooming. When conditions are right, plants look healthy and happy.
Top: Heterocentron roseum.
Left: A colorful array including Tulipa, Hyacinthus, *and* Camellia.

Striking a Balance

The benefits and problems of a heated greenhouse can be summarized as follows.

1. A warmer greenhouse accommodates a wider range of plant species, and in addition tends to be more comfortable for the gardener.

2. A warmer greenhouse hastens the maturation of a plant, but may reduce the length of its flowering period once it has reached maturity.

3. A warmer greenhouse results in greater water uptake by the plants because of both lower humidity and higher metabolic activity. This can subject plants to drought stress.

4. Arthropod pests (insects and spider mites) are more of a problem in a warmer greenhouse.

There are two general ways of balancing these realities, depending on the gardener's individual goals. A gardener who prefers to have a warmer greenhouse, perhaps to grow a particular group of plants, can counter problems of lower humidity and increased pest activity by paying more attention to watering, humidifying, and pest suppression.

An alternative approach is to operate the greenhouse at a lower temperature, letting that minimum temperature dictate the plants that can be grown. This may mean that the greenhouse will not be very comfortable part of the time, especially at night and on cloudy days. On the other hand, as the minimum temperature approaches or goes below the freezing point, pests will become dormant or be killed outright, the relative humidity will be higher, and the plants, given that they are adapted to the temperature, will pass the winter in pristine condition.

The Subfreezing Greenhouse

For many species, such as *Camellia japonica*, there is nothing magical about 32° F. Other species, such as *Aloe affinis* and *Tibouchina urvilleana*, may be killed outright at the

Not every greenhouse gardener is looking for a display of flowers. Foliage plants and trees are often combined to produce a lush and inviting setting. A few flowering plants can be added to provide splashes of color.

freezing point, although they may remain untouched just a degree or two higher. Still others, such as *Clerodendron* species or *Strelitzia reginae*, may not succeed at temperatures below 40°, 50°, or even 60° F. The point is that a subfreezing greenhouse is different in degree, not in kind. It will provide the same gardening pleasures as a more typical greenhouse but with a different array of species.

An abundance of species grow well as long as the minimum temperature in the greenhouse is above 12° F, and many of these hardy plants will bloom in winter.

Hardiness, the ability of an organism to endure cold, is generally expressed as the minimum winter temperature the species can withstand. The degree of hardiness is primarily a matter of genetic makeup. It differs from species to species and, to a lesser extent, among individuals and populations within a species. Species as a whole are given hardiness ratings expressed in terms of the coldest climatic zone in which they can survive (see map, page 36), but these ratings are not to be taken so seriously as to exclude experimentation. Populations from higher altitudes or latitudes are well worth trying, for instance, and in any case hardiness has a somewhat different meaning in a greenhouse than it has outside, because of the absence of the damaging effects of air motion.

Hardiness is also affected by cultural techniques. Hardening off prepares a plant for subfreezing temperatures by exposing it for a period of several weeks to levels below about 40° F (which, of course, happens naturally in the course of autumn in many temperate zones). In addition, plants that are well grown and healthy will be more cold-resistant.

It goes almost without saying that a subfreezing greenhouse is a strictly solar-heated one, with no supplemental heat. Among other advantages, a solar-heated greenhouse is particularly good for growing plants in the ground, and it can be designed for complete disassembly in the summer to provide total ventilation. A greenhouse designed for disassembly is likely to leak more than one that is conventionally designed, and so is more costly if fossil fuels are involved. So long as such a greenhouse is solar-heated, all that is lost are a few degrees of minimum temperature.

The greenhouse environment gives the gardener the opportunity to choose and to experiment. Countless plant species from around the world are available and easy to grow indoors.
Bottom right: Oxalis versicolor.
Opposite, top: Pelargonium echinatum.
Opposite, bottom: Abutilon hybridum.

USES OF THE GREENHOUSE

The all-purpose climate of the greenhouse can be put to any number of uses besides growing a range of ornamentals. The most frequent are food production, horticultural specializations, decoration of the home, and solar heating.

Food Production

The environment of the greenhouse is in many ways well suited to food production. The major problem the gardener faces is how to control pests and still have a pesticide-free product. Be aware at the outset that the average greenhouse is not a cost-effective environment in which to raise food, though a large solar-heated greenhouse might come close. In general, the plot of land enclosed in a greenhouse is no more productive on a year-to-year basis than it would be if left unenclosed, and of course there will be many additional expenses. There are, however, excellent reasons to use the greenhouse for food plants: absolute freshness, freedom from contaminants, and the possibility of growing exotic varieties.

Many fruits and vegetables grow well in a greenhouse environment. Eating what you've grown is always a thrill, especially in the cold winter months when interesting produce is scarce. Exotic crops that are not generally sold in the markets are often available as seeds or plants.

Vegetables, fruits, and herbs can all be successfully grown in a greenhouse. Among vegetables, off-season crops are of most interest. (Summertime crops will be difficult to achieve in any case because of the high heat in the greenhouse then.) The tomato tends to have the most appeal to gardeners, although it is less suited to greenhouse cultivation than many other plants. Nonetheless, tomatoes of good quality are grown commercially in greenhouses, and varieties such as 'Kito' have been developed specifically for greenhouse cultivation. Cherry tomatoes are somewhat hardier and in general better able to withstand less than optimum watering, feeding, soil, and other conditions and may therefore be a better choice. 'Tiny Tim' has the additional advantage of being dwarf.

Other warm-temperature vegetables to consider are cucumber ('La Reine' was bred for greenhouse growing); eggplant (the Japanese Nasu types are small and quite compact); melons such as 'Doan Gwa' and 'Ha-ogen'; and for something different, the sweet potato,

A citrus tree provides a foliage backdrop for the more dramatic Kalanchoe pumila. When its fruit is ready for picking, however, the tree claims the spotlight.

which enjoys the warmth if it isn't destroyed by whiteflies. Whiteflies, mealybugs, and aphids are indeed particular threats to all these vegetables, whose natural defenses have largely been sacrificed for other properties.

Other vegetables, such as beans, beets, brassicas (including cabbage, brussels sprouts, and cauliflower), celery, chard, and leeks, can certainly be grown in a greenhouse too. In fact, they are a good deal more cold tolerant than cucumbers, eggplant, melons, and sweet potatoes; some species and varieties can tolerate temperatures well below freezing. But they are all readily available in good condition at all times, and can as well be grown in a simple cold frame. A less well-known vegetable that is worth growing is cornsalad (*Valerianella locusta*), a winter-growing green that is quick from seed, very hardy, and has a distinctive taste in a salad. Varieties are 'Duplex' and 'Verte de Cambrai'.

Fruit-bearing trees and shrubs have many characteristics in their favor: they are ornamental, perennial, tough, and in many cases bear fruits that are not readily available at the supermarket, although that is rapidly

changing. They also tend to grow quite large, however small they may be at the beginning of bearing. In the "Plant Directory" that begins on page 43 are listed *Ananas comosus* (pineapple); *Citrus*; *Eriobotrya japonica* (loquat); *Eugenia uniflora* (Surinam-cherry); *Feijoa sellowiana* (pineapple guava); *Fortunella* (kumquat); *Malpighia glabra* (Barbadoscherry); *Passiflora quadrangularis* (giant granadilla, or passionfruit); and *Psidium cattleianum* and *P. guajava* (strawberry guava and guava). Not included are *Actinidia chinensis* (kiwifruit), which is decorative and very hardy but too large, and *Ficus carica* (fig) and *Physalis peruviana* (groundcherry), which have too small a fruit-to-foliage ratio.

There are not many herbs, in the narrow sense of plants with leaves used in cooking, that are suitable for the greenhouse. Described in the "Plant Directory" are *Eucalyptus, Pelargonium,* and *Rosmarinus.* The flowers of *Jasminum officinale* can be used to flavor tea. Certainly hardier herbs such as thyme can be brought inside, but they are more at home outdoors and do not tend to grow well under such soft conditions.

Decoration of the Home

Plants can be grown in a greenhouse to a degree of perfection not easy to achieve in the house itself. It is natural to want to show them off to best advantage by bringing them inside. Transferring plants from greenhouse to house does present some problems, however (see page 41). The length of time a greenhouse plant stays in the house must be limited or all the advantages of having been grown in a greenhouse will be lost.

One area in which the change of environment need not be of great concern is in the forcing of bulbs, particularly if the bulbs are to be discarded after they flower. To force a bulb it is only necessary to expose it to an amount of cold or dryness or both that convinces the bulb it has gone through a summer and perhaps part of a winter. A colder greenhouse may do this automatically; for warmer greenhouses, the bulbs should be prechilled by the supplier or by the gardener.

Bulbs for forcing do not need a period of residency in a greenhouse; started in a greenhouse, however, they can be brought along in more sparkling condition. They can be shared between the greenhouse and the house when in flower, and with minimal care can be grown on for another year of bloom. If the plants are kept entirely in the greenhouse, blooms last longer, and stay in better shape. See "Bulbs for Forcing" (page 55).

Horticultural Specializations

The greenhouse is a perfect place to bring similar kinds of plants together in a collection—plants in the same family or genus, plants with the same cultural requirements, or plants that have the same aesthetic impact. The most common such groupings are alpines, begonias, bromeliads, gesneriads, orchids, and succulents.

Alpines will do best in a cold, bright environment and are most likely to be grown in a

There is often a great deal of variation among the species of a particular genus. Several species of one genus grown together can make a fascinating display.
Left: Salvia guaranitica.
Bottom left: Salvia clevelandii.
Bottom right: Salvia greggii.

solar-heated greenhouse. Begonias and ges-neriads share a need for both warmth and shade from the summer sun. Bromeliads and orchids, as grown by most fanciers, are epiphytes; both require a fibrous, free-drain-ing growing medium. Bromeliad and orchid species run the gamut of temperature toler-ance, from near freezing to a minimum tem-perature of 50° F or more. Bromeliads prefer a good deal more summer sunlight than most orchids. Of all these groups, succulents are best suited to the greenhouse. They accept the extremes of temperature day and night, sum-mer and winter, are unaffected by the some-times very low humidity, and are able to withstand a good deal of neglect.

Opposite: An attached greenhouse is a source of passive solar heating as well as a pleasant setting for conversation or reading.
Bottom: The pleasures of greenhouse gardening speak for themselves in the eloquence of a perfect flower. Pelargonium *is one of the most popular greenhouse plants; the radiant 'Prairie Dawn' shows why.*

Solar Heating

An attached home greenhouse can readily serve as a source of passive solar heating, if there is an opening between house and greenhouse large enough to permit some diffusion of heat. The benefits will be modest, however, unless more active steps are taken, primarily by forcing the heated air from greenhouse to house with a fan or other type of air circulator. In any case, there is not likely to be a significant surplus of warmth before the first of March or after the middle of October, although that surplus can be ample and welcome in March, April, and May.

Exhausting the heat into the house also serves to ventilate and cool the greenhouse to some extent, but to be at all useful in the warmer months the exhaust system would have to be powerful and include some type of heat storage in the house. Circulating air between the greenhouse and the house may lower the humidity of the greenhouse and raise the humidity of the house, but the effect is not likely to be pronounced enough in either location to make a significant difference.

THE GREENHOUSE AND THE GARDENER

Overall, a greenhouse fits the requirements of plants closely, but they will thrive only with help from the gardener. The need for light is met by the nature of the structure. Some warmth comes with the light; it may be enough in itself or may need to be supplemented, depending on the goals of the gardener. But hard on the heels of the warmth comes too much of it, and here the gardener must intervene. Options for reducing heat include shading, ventilation (even to the extent of removing all overhead glazing for the summer), and moving potted plants outdoors.

There are many essential tasks that go along with greenhouse gardening, including watering, fertilizing, and pest control. The amount of effort you put in, above and beyond some essential minimum, is up to you. By expending a reasonable effort and learning to work with the greenhouse environment, you will be able to create a distinctive indoor garden of exotic plants, glowing with flowers and foliage on even the bleakest winter days.

Caring for Greenhouse Plants

A wide variety of plants will thrive in the warm, sunny atmosphere of a greenhouse, asking only an appropriate growing medium and a standard program of watering, feeding, and pest control.

G ardening in a greenhouse involves the same concerns as gardening outdoors—light, warmth, soil, water, feeding, pests, and propagation—though in somewhat different proportions. To ensure healthy, attractive plants, these concerns must be addressed, but this need not be an onerous task.

Automating ventilation, watering, and even feeding can reduce the drudgery, and pest problems can be overcome by choosing resistant plants, operating at low temperatures, introducing predators, or applying pesticides. Automation, however, is based on the assumption that all the species in the greenhouse can be cared for according to some standard routine, as if they all belonged to a single, well-understood species. Fortunately, thanks in large part to the forgiving nature of most plants, a large number of greenhouse plants can adapt to such a routine. Given a minimum of four hours of midday sun (direct or lightly shaded), a well-drained, noncompacting growing medium, copious water in summer and relatively dry conditions in winter, and some feeding, a wide variety of plants will grow and flower.

Many—perhaps most—of the plants described in the "Plant Directory" beginning on page 43 will thrive with the standard culture techniques discussed in this chapter. Unusual requirements are spelled out where appropriate.

The routines of caring for greenhouse plants are generally simple; the rewards are great. Here in his splendid retreat, surrounded by his favorite colors and aromas, a gardener tends an orchid in bloom. The more time a gardener spends caring for a private oasis, the more it flourishes.

CULTURE

The feeding and watering requirements of
plants are different in summer and winter, or,
more precisely, in active-growing and dormant periods. What this means in terms of
actual months of the year varies according to
the climatic zone and the minimum temperature of a given greenhouse as well as the species grown. In general, it is safe to say that
dormancy for summer-active plants does not
begin before the middle of November and ends
close to the middle of February.

Growing Medium

Plain soil, such as loam taken from the garden, does not in general do very well in a
greenhouse. Earthworms and other agents
that work to loosen the soil outside do not
seem to function effectively inside, particularly in pots. Without their help, the soil com-
pacts with time, hindering penetration by
roots, nutrients, and water and seriously af-
fecting the growth of the plant.

Loam can, however, serve as a satisfactory
base if it is screened to remove rocks and
other debris and is opened up with peat moss
and perlite or vermiculite, two parts loam to
one part of each of the other ingredients. Or
the loam can be omitted altogether, the medium then consisting only of perlite or vermiculite and peat moss. Many growers find
this even more effective, but such a medium
requires much more attention to watering and
feeding since it contains no nutrients whatso-
ever and does not show the visible changes
that signal dryness in a loam-based medium.
Such a "soilless" medium is most appropriate
for seedlings (though seedlings do not in general require it), for plants of unusual diffi-
culty, and for commercial growers who want
quick growth and can provide the needed attention. A loam-based medium is preferable
for the more casual gardener who has a range
of more standard plants.

Garden loam is often full of weed seeds and
may also harbor disease organisms. If loam is
used for sowing seeds, the weeds will quickly
swamp the seedlings. Loam can be sterilized
by heating it in the oven at 350° F for 45 min-
utes (some people don't at all like the odor) or
by using a sterilizing chemical. The only fumi-
gant available to home gardeners for this purpose is metham (Vapam®), which requires a

period of two to three weeks to dissipate after
application (it should be applied outdoors).
Use easily germinating seeds to test the soil's
readiness before sowing more valuable ones.

Watering

Plants in a greenhouse, shut off from natural
precipitation, need help from the gardener.
The frequency with which potted plants need
to be watered varies with the season, the species of plant, the water retention of the growing medium, and the ratio of foliage mass to
medium mass. Greenhouse plants growing in
the ground are much less demanding than
those in pots, but they nonetheless require
more water than outdoor plants in the ground
because the temperature inside is always
somewhat higher.

Even in greenhouses where the overhead
panes are removed for the summer, plants in

*Regular watering is
essential in the
greenhouse. Plants
indoors require more
water than those
growing outside. It is
important to be aware
of the watering needs
of various plants
in different seasons
and to establish a
schedule for meeting
those needs.*

the ground need more supplemental watering than do those outside, again because of the temperature differential and because any remaining glazing acts as a heat trap. The quick-draining nature of the medium also causes it to dry out more rapidly.

In summer an average plant in a pot of proper proportions is likely to need watering every two or three days if outside and daily if in the greenhouse. The same plant could go two to three weeks between waterings in a cool greenhouse in winter. In summer it is difficult to overwater most species of plants, even succulents, as long as the growing medium drains well. In winter the reverse is true; most species should be watered sparingly. The cooler the conditions, the less frequently plants need water.

What about spring and fall? In a greenhouse, those seasons occur only fleetingly, if at all. For cultural operations such as feeding and watering, the year is divided into only two seasons: From mid-February to mid-November it is summer, and from mid-November to mid-February is winter. However, the summertime routine is not uniform throughout the period. The high demand for feeding and watering in the ear-lier months, as the sun is waxing, tapers off by mid-September, after which feeding, in most cases, is no longer desirable and watering requirements gradually approach the winter minimum.

Fertilizer

Species of plants vary tremendously in their need for supplemental nutrients. The exact requirements for a given species are not in general well known, but few species are injured by a standard feeding regimen. Even plants that are relatively self-sufficient, such as members of the pea family (Leguminosae), which have nitrogen-fixing bacteria living symbiotically on their roots, do well with standard feeding. Nonetheless, whatever specific information on feeding requirements is available is included in the "Plant Directory," which begins on page 43.

There are factors other than the needs of the plant that affect the standard feeding regimen, notably the type of fertilizer used and the needs of the gardener.

Types of fertilizer The major elements that must be supplied to plants are nitrogen (N),

Most greenhouse plants can be grown with a standard program of watering and feeding. There are some exceptions, however. Plants in pots need to be watered more often than plants in the ground. And certain species have special needs. It is wise to group plants with similar needs together.

Regular applications of fertilizer help most plants to reach their full size and produce an abundance of blooms. During the growing season, fertilizer should be applied twice a week. No fertilizer is needed at times of the year when a plant is not growing.

phosphorus (P), and potassium (K). A host of necessary trace elements are almost certainly provided by a loam-based medium.

Nitrogen stimulates shoot and leaf growth and chlorophyll development; it is the most likely nutrient to be in short supply. Phosphorus encourages strong root formation and stimulates flowering and setting of fruit. Potassium is important for general vigor and for increasing resistance to disease, insects, and extremes of temperature.

Most commercial fertilizers include all three basic elements. The percentage of each in a given fertilizer is noted on the label, with the elements always listed in the same order. A fertilizer marked 5-10-5 contains 5 percent nitrogen, 10 percent phosphorus, and 5 percent potassium, and is probably intended for fruit plants.

"Natural" or unprocessed fertilizers include greensand to provide phosphorous, potassium, and trace minerals; bone meal for phosphorus; and dried animal manure for nitrogen and the general improvement of soil structure known as tilth. These release their nutrients slowly and are less concentrated than commercial fertilizers. Because of this there is no danger of chemical burning of the plant roots, but the supply of nutrients may be

insufficient, particularly for potted plants, and will certainly be slower acting.

The standard feeding regimen referred to throughout this book is a twice-weekly application of a soluble fertilizer formulated for use with potted plants during the growing season (mid-February to mid-September) and none at all at other times. An alternative approach is to apply a slow-release fertilizer once a year, preferably at the time of spring repotting. Once-a-year fertilizing is certainly more convenient, but it is less effective in producing immediate results and, as with "natural" fertilizers, may not be enough for a plant's needs.

The needs of the gardener What most greenhouse gardeners want is to bring each plant to a peak of perfection—filled out, of an appreciable size, and in full bloom—and hold it there. Continuing growth may heighten the impact of a plant, but after a certain point it only leads to awkwardness as the plant becomes too large to move about and claims more than its share of greenhouse space.

Many of the species described in this book are naturally small; for them, growth usually means an increase in the number of separate plantlets, which can be divided and potted up separately (but still must be put somewhere). A number of desirable woody plants, however, are quite large in nature and will probably outgrow the greenhouse in time. How long that takes is the important factor. If it is 10 or 15 years, then the investment can be well worthwhile.

With large plants, then, the goal of the greenhouse gardener is to slow growth as much as possible. That means using the minimum amount of fertilizer, enough to keep the plant healthy and flowering, but no more. The standard feeding regimen should therefore be tapered off as the plant reaches maturity and followed by a more experimental approach. Watch for signs of starvation: leaf yellowing and loss, susceptibility to pests, and reduced flowering.

GREENHOUSE PESTS

It is just about inevitable that a greenhouse will be affected by pests of one sort or another. The effects range from slight disfigurement to unsightly infestations to outright death of the affected plants. A number of pests can infiltrate a greenhouse, but by and large the most serious ones are four species of arthropods: whitefly (*Trialeurodes vaporarium*); aphid (*Myzas persica*), called greenfly by the English; mealybug (*Pseudococcus* species); and spider mite (*Tetranychus urticae*). Measures taken to control these four are generally effective against other species as well.

The gardener's weapons include chemicals that interfere with the life processes of the pests; biological controls, which are often other, predatory arthropods; various mechanical techniques; and, most effective of all, choosing resistant species and strains of plants and maintaining their health through good culture.

If used rigorously enough, chemical pesticides can clean out a greenhouse so thoroughly that no signs of pests remain. Biological agents, on the other hand, are never 100 percent effective; they themselves would be likely to die out if they were. Nonetheless, they can keep infestation levels low enough to protect the plants and prevent eyesores.

Most chemical pesticides are effective against a wide range of pests. Pesticides used on a large scale therefore control all the common arthropods in a greenhouse, but they kill beneficial arthropods as well. Large-scale use of chemicals may be harmful to humans or to other animals, such as fish or birds, that might be kept in the greenhouse, and is inadvisable if edible plants are being grown. It is best to use pesticides along with other methods of control, applying them locally to spot infestations. It is very important to read and heed the instructions and warnings for each product.

Biological and mechanical controls are more pest specific. Recommendations for their use, as well as for the appropriate chemical controls, are included in the following discussions of the pests themselves.

Whiteflies

Powdery white and very small though quite visible, whiteflies congregate on the undersides of leaves where their crawling larvae do great damage by sucking the plant juices. Their presence is readily diagnosed; swarms of them appear if the leaf is disturbed, and in a heavy infestation there is a constant coming and going between plants.

They can multiply at a very high rate, and in large numbers whiteflies seriously weaken the plants. Heavily infested plants will suffer retarded growth, yellowing or mottled foliage, and drastically reduced flowering.

The most widely used biological opponent of whitefly is *Encarsia formosa*, a barely visible wasp that parasitizes the larvae of the fly. These tiny wasps are available commercially (see "Insectaries," page 108) and should be

A leaf infested with whiteflies. The larvae of whiteflies suck juices from leaves, causing slower plant growth and greatly reduced flowering.

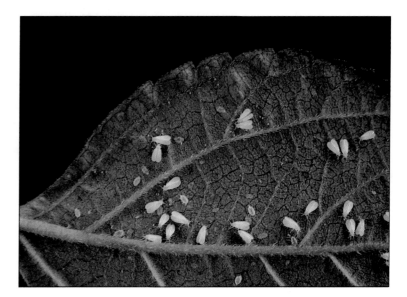

purchased in early spring when a whitefly explosion is most likely to begin and before the greenhouse ventilators are opened (as the wasps may escape). When warm weather arrives and the greenhouse is opened up, local predatory insects move in and take up the task. Some may in fact establish a toehold in a diversified greenhouse, but *E. formosa* will probably die out.

Insects are not the only ones that eat whiteflies. Finches, especially zebra finches, can keep whitefly levels satisfactorily low, even when they are not allowed to move around within the greenhouse. Whiteflies are apparently mobile enough that sooner or later they come to the birds. These birds can readily endure temperatures down to 32° F.

Some mechanical controls are also effective against whitefly. An easy, passive approach is to hang out special traps for whiteflies—sticky cards with a yellow surface that attracts the flies. This method may be of only limited effectiveness, however; it is an area of continuing experimentation. A more active, immediately effective approach when faced with a large population of whiteflies is to shake the leaves and vacuum up the cloud of flies.

Chemical control is complicated to some extent by the fact that different stages of the whitefly life cycle are susceptible to different pesticides; some stages are not susceptible to any at all. A malathion spray will wipe out the nymph stage. A spray containing Orthene® acts as a systemic as well as a contact poison, and is effective for the stage that succeeds the nymph, when the insect is in a legless, scale-like form. The adult flying stage can be attacked with pyrethrins or resmethrin-petroleum oil spray.

Aphids

Multiplying even faster than whiteflies, aphids are active at cooler temperatures. Fortunately, they concentrate on just the tender new leaves and shoots.

They are easily recognized; look for small, soft-bodied insects, wingless or winged, green or brown, clustered at the ends of the shoots. Their damage can go beyond weakening the plant they feed on. A substance called honeydew which they exude encourages black sooty mold and other fungi when it drips on leaves. The black sooty mold doesn't directly hurt the

plant, but it is unsightly and can interfere with photosynthesis. The honeydew also attracts ants, which prize it so highly that they protect and "milk" the aphids that produce it. Their protection is significant enough that an important step in controlling aphids is to control the ants first, which can be done readily and safely with ant traps or with an ant-killing powder.

Aphids are prey to a large number of insects. Among the most effective is the lacewing (*Chrysopidae*), which is effective both as larva and adult and is available from insectaries (see page 108). Also available are the parasite *Aphidius matricariae* and the ladybug beetle, though the latter has gotten mixed

Aphids attack tender new leaves and shoots. Fortunately, several easily obtainable insects prey on them. Top: The lacewing is an effective control. Bottom: Another hungry predator, the ladybug, devours aphids on a leaf.

reviews, largely because it is usually gathered at a dispersive phase of its life. Local predators include braconid and chalcid wasps, both minute parasitizers; robber flies; gnats, and a fungus that specializes in aphids.

The larva of the fly *Aphidoletes aphidimyza* is an important natural enemy; it may be found as a speck of orange on milkweed leaves in the fall and brought, leaf and all, into the greenhouse. Place the leaf near a plant sporting or likely to sport an aphid infestation and let nature take its course.

Birds will pick over plants that are introduced into their cage and consume aphids. Infested shoots can also be snapped off and thrown to the fish in a greenhouse that has a pond. The gardener who has the time and inclination can squash a heavy infestation by sliding two fingers along affected shoots—a messy but effective method.

Chemical control of aphids is straightforward. They are vulnerable to just about any general-purpose house and greenhouse pesticide spray, specifically one containing Orthene®, resmethrin, malathion, or pyrethrin. It may be desirable to go to the source by using diazinon granules, which attack the ants that nurture the aphids.

Mealybugs

A gardener who uses biological controls must accept the fact there will always be residual populations of pests. This philosophy of tolerance is strained by the mealybug. These grayish white (orange when crushed) insects form masses so unsightly as to completely ruin the appeal of a plant. They are very destructive, stunting growth and disfiguring foliage as they suck out a plant's juices.

Mealybugs are found most frequently in leaf axils (the angles between the leaves and the supporting branches or stems), on the undersides of leaves, and clustered around the stems of fruit. They favor some species far more than others. They are sensitive to cold, so are a minor nuisance in a cool greenhouse.

The biological controls applied to aphids also have some impact on mealybugs, but the most effective control is a beetle, *Cryptolaemus montrouzerieri*, that is available from insectaries (see page 108) and is adapted to higher temperatures.

Spot infestations of mealybugs can be eliminated by dabbing the insects with a cotton swab dipped in alcohol, which kills them promptly. Mealybugs are protected to some extent against chemical pesticides by their waxy coating. This can be overcome by using a systemic pesticide such as Orthene® or an oil spray; general-purpose sprays containing malathion are also effective, if carefully applied.

Spider Mites

The cool, damp conditions of a cooler greenhouse do not encourage these nearly invisible relatives of the spider, but they can be major pests in a warm, dry greenhouse, or in any warm, dry microclimate within a greenhouse, such as close to the glazing. Infested plants have yellowed, brittle-looking leaves traced with silky strands; they are seriously weakened and their growth is retarded.

Spider mites are not a great problem in a cool greenhouse, but they frequently infest heated greenhouses, seriously weakening the plants they attack.

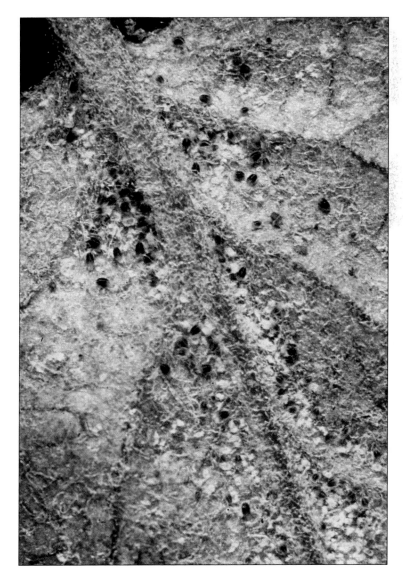

Scale can be a problem in a warm greenhouse. It attacks only susceptible plants, such as Camellia *(right),* Citrus, *and* Ardisia.

The best control is eliminating the conditions that breed the mites by adjusting temperature and humidity. This can be accomplished by routinely spraying with water, as much as once a day during sunny periods.

A predatory mite, *Phytoseilus persimilis*, also available from insectaries, controls spider mites with great success, but populations are not likely to endure once they have reduced their prey below a certain level.

Mites seem innately to be more resistant to chemical controls than are many other pests; their eggs in particular are very difficult to kill. Products containing Vendex™ are effective, however, as is an oil spray. A spray containing Orthene® and resmethrin will give good results if conscientiously applied. A minimum of three applications at 7- to 10-day intervals is necessary to catch successive hatchings.

Secondary Pests

Scale, a soft-bodied insect that is enclosed by a small but readily visible one-sided shell, is not uncommon in greenhouses, but it appears to require relatively warm conditions and to be limited to susceptible species, *Citrus* and *Ardisia* being notable examples. Localized infestations are easily wiped off with an alcohol-soaked swab, and biological control is

available in the form of *Aphytis melimus*, a parasitizing wasp, which is available from insectaries. Widespread infestations may require a systemic insecticide, which is added to the soil and taken up by the plant through its roots, making the sap poisonous. Di-syston® works in this way as well as on contact. Resmethrin is also effective, as is exposure to outdoor predators.

Slugs and snails are omnipresent outdoors and are likely to show up in the greenhouse as well. For most plants this is a matter of little concern, but when it comes to vulnerable species slugs are unerring and voracious. Many solutions have been proposed. A saucer of beer, set out as an irresistible and fatal lure, and ashes spread about to repel the pests have been reported successful. The best defense is good housekeeping—elimination of the litter that gives them shelter. Biological controls for slugs are particularly appealing: toads and glowworms (the larvae of fireflies). Chemical controls are generally available in the form of baits containing metaldehyde or methiocarb. Be sure that pets or children cannot get at the bait.

Thrips are tiny, active insects that may sometimes build up in damaging numbers. They are controlled by the same predators and pesticides that control aphids.

DISEASES AND FUNGI

Both diseases and fungi are primarily the result of poor greenhouse-keeping, specifically overdampness caused by overwatering or excessive humidity, accumulations of leaf litter and other debris, weakening of plants by inadequate watering or feeding, or infestations of aphids or other sap-sucking pests that may open up pathways of infection.

If none of these conditions exist, neither disease nor fungus is likely to be a major problem, and any outbreak can usually be controlled by greater attention to the plants' needs. A persistent or widespread fungal attack calls for a fungicide such as captan or chlorothalonil. Affected plant parts should be pruned off and removed from the greenhouse; in some cases this may mean the whole infected plant.

Leaf Spot

Fungi or bacteria that are carried by splashed water can cause a condition called leaf spot. It appears as dark spots on the foliage, possibly causing the leaf itself to brown and droop. Roses are quite susceptible; others that may occasionally be affected are azaleas, begonias, and chrysanthemums. Leaf spot can be prevented by careful watering to avoid leaf splash. It is best to restrict overhead watering to the morning if any plants show spotting.

Mildew

Most gardeners are probably familiar with mildew, a fuzzy gray-white coating on the leaves and stems of chrysanthemums, roses, and other susceptible plants. Such plants should be kept out of cool, dark, damp situations. Remove affected parts of the plant, and spray with a fungicide such as triforine if an outbreak cannot be controlled by lowering humidity and increasing ventilation.

Botrytis

A cold, damp atmosphere and poor ventilation can lead to botrytis. Botrytis causes small, brown rotted spots on leaves, flowers, or stems and is most likely to attack such bulbous plants as lilies, narcissi, and tulips; peonies are also susceptible. Remove infected leaves promptly and, most importantly, improve the growing conditions. If ventilation cannot be improved, the best approach may be not to choose susceptible species in the first place. A fungicide such as chlorothalonil may also help.

Top right: Leaf spot can cause leaves to turn brown and droop. Caused by fungi or bacteria in splashed water, it can be avoided by careful watering.
Bottom right: Mildew on a squash plant.
Bottom left: Botrytis on petunia flowers.

Damping-off

When visible at all, damping-off looks like a sparse kind of mildew. It is caused by an omnipresent fungus that can cut down a bed of seedlings overnight. It is easily avoided by sterilizing the planting medium, which should be done in any case. Damping-off, once it has occurred, can be controlled with a fungicide such as captan. Only seedlings appear to be vulnerable, and those primarily when grown in a close, humid atmosphere.

Other Problems

Greenhouse plants also fall victim to root rot, or wilt, or become stunted, or deformed. The first three result from poor drainage. Drainage can be improved by opening up the planting medium (see page 26) or choosing a container that drains better, but it is unlikely that an individual plant showing those symptoms can be saved. Plants that are stunted or show misshapen leaf growth are most likely infected with a virus and should be promptly discarded.

PROPAGATION

Most greenhouse gardeners enjoy propagation of plants if for no other reason than that the environment is so favorable for it. The greenhouse provides a controlled and predictable climate; protection from wind, rain, cats, dogs, and other destructive elements; comfortable access whatever the weather outside; and a range of temperatures and light levels to suit various species and propagation methods. Propagation also allows the gardener to acquire rare or expensive plants, build up a large collection of a given species, or perpetuate plants on hand that are particularly desirable or that need periodic renewing.

There are two types of propagation: sexual and vegetative. Sexual propagation is based on seeds (or spores). Since seeds in general combine characteristics from two different parent plants, they can produce variation in the resulting offspring. In vegetative propagation, on the other hand, tissue from a growing plant is induced to take on a separate existence; the offspring are identical to the original plant in all characteristics. Vegetative techniques include cuttings, layering, division, and grafting.

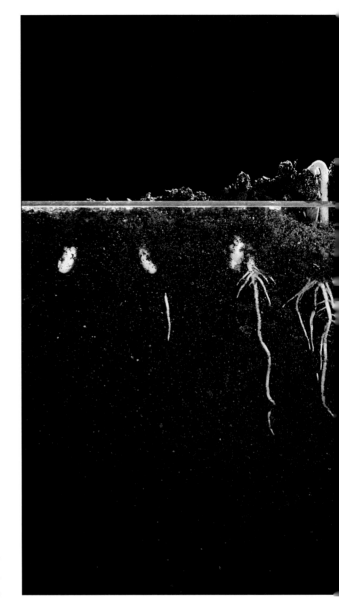

Seeds

There are several reasons for propagating by seeds. It allows a gardener to acquire species that are not available any other way. Most seeds can be shipped without restriction across national boundaries (as can dormant bulbs, corms, and tubers), whereas live plants require special handling and, for some species, government permits. Propagation by seeds also makes it possible for the gardener to acquire a number of the same species cheaply, to explore genetic variability, to gain a more intimate knowledge of a species' cultural requirements, and to enjoy the seed sowing and growing process.

Seeds of different species may have quite different environmental requirements, such as needs for light or darkness, for warmth or

Planting seeds is usually the least expensive way of starting new plants. There is a certain excitement in watching a seedling push through the soil, straighten up, and begin to grow.

dark conditions and, equally important, will serve to prevent the growth of moss, which can be a nuisance. Seeds in the dark should be checked every day or two to prevent recently germinated seedlings from becoming too elongated or whitened (etiolated) in their search for light. It is not unreasonable to keep seed trays for two years or more. Keep them in the light most of the time (particularly in the spring); move them to dark conditions only when moss begins to appear.

Sowing begins with the preparation of a sterilized medium (see page 26). Place the sterilized medium in a pot or seed tray and moisten thoroughly. The seeds may be sown directly on top of the soil; larger seeds should be covered lightly. The container should be carefully labeled; many growers also find it useful to keep records of sowing and germination times. Put the container in a location appropriate to the species. Whether light or dark, warm or cold, the location should be humid and shielded from direct sunlight. Once seedlings have appeared they can be exposed to more intense light, the amount depending on the species.

Seedlings should be left in the container until they are well established and large enough to be handled, which is generally considered to be when the first true leaves appear. (Seedlings initially have a pair of round, generalized seed-leaves.) However, transplanting at a somewhat earlier stage is also likely to be successful.

Once seedlings reach a proper size, the next step is to prick them out—that is, to remove them one by one from the seedling container into seed flats in which they can be spaced a comfortable distance apart. Vigorous species, such as many of the annuals (*Calendula, Tagetes erecta*), *Agapanthus, Eucalyptus,* and *Gerbera,* as well as such large-seeded species as *Camellia, Citrus, Eriobotrya,* and *Strelitzia,* can be moved directly from the flats into individual pots or garden beds. Wait until they are 2 or 3 inches tall, so that they will not subsequently be overlooked and neglected.

Slower growing groups, such as *Begonia, Crossandra,* gesneriads, salvias, and the succulents, may need an intermediate stage, such as an outside nursery bed over the summer. A nursery bed permits continuing observation but cuts down on the amount of

cold, that may or may not be explained on the seed packet. Most species germinate well under light conditions; some absolutely require such conditions. There is a greater split when it comes to temperature. Many temperate species require a stratification period near or below freezing to break the cold-dormancy of a seed whereas warmer-region seeds may be injured by low temperatures (probably only below freezing, however).

It is a good idea to stratify the seeds of all temperate-zone species by exposing them to temperatures below 40° F for six to eight weeks, whether they need it or not. Sow all seeds in light; transfer any that don't germinate within three above-freezing months to the dark. Putting them in the dark will enhance the germination of any species that require

Climate Zone Map

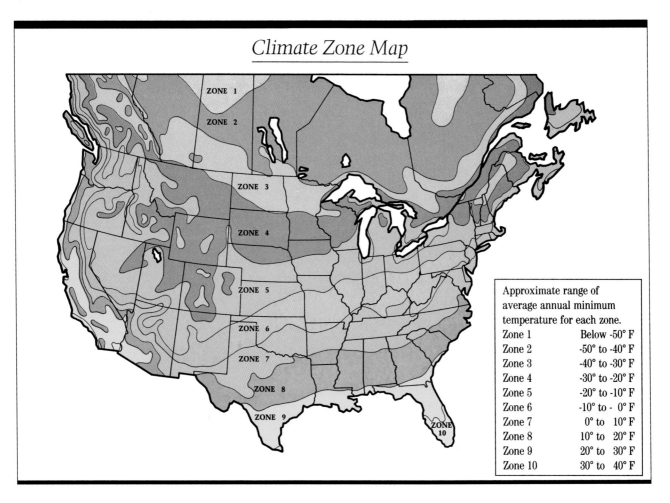

Approximate range of average annual minimum temperature for each zone.

Zone 1	Below -50° F
Zone 2	-50° to -40° F
Zone 3	-40° to -30° F
Zone 4	-30° to -20° F
Zone 5	-20° to -10° F
Zone 6	-10° to - 0° F
Zone 7	0° to 10° F
Zone 8	10° to 20° F
Zone 9	20° to 30° F
Zone 10	30° to 40° F

Opposite, top: The temperature inside an unheated greenhouse drops in response to the temperature outside in winter. Choose plants that can tolerate the expected greenhouse winter temperatures in your area. The climate zone map shows the approximate average minimum temperature for each zone. Opposite, bottom: Orchids, such as Dendrobium, *can be propagated by seeds or by division. Right: Orchid seeds and pod.*

care, primarily watering, that is needed. Certainly, those seedlings that are less than ¼-inch tall at the beginning of summer should be put in a nursery bed.

The time it takes a plant to grow from seedling to flowering size varies from several months to five or more years, depending on the species and the cultural methods used.

Cuttings

Most species of woody plants as well as many soft-stemmed ones can be propagated by cuttings. Exceptions include *Eucalyptus* and *Fortunella hindsii*, as well as many of the hardy stone fruits. Some genera, such as *Leucadendron* and *Protea*, take root much more slowly than others and may require special techniques, such as misting or use of a rooting hormone. For other plants, including azalea, citrus, camellia, eugenia, and guava, the hormone is not necessary but may speed up the process.

The great majority of species will respond to this simple method: Take cuttings from late spring through early summer. Each cutting should be a piece of stem or branch, ½ inch to 3 inches in length and less than ¼ inch thick at the base, cut cleanly from the parent plant. Make sure each cutting includes two or three leaves. The length of the cutting depends to some extent on the size of the parent species.

Dip the cutting in a rooting hormone, if desired. This may speed the rooting process and perhaps induce some difficult species to root, but in general it does not seem to be necessary. Place the cuttings in a loose, water-retentive medium, such as a mixture of sand and peat moss, in a humid, enclosed environment, such as a cold-frame, that is bright but does not receive direct sun. The north side of a house, greenhouse, or fence is a perfect location. Keep the medium moist and check the cuttings at intervals to see if roots have formed.

Some growers leave the cuttings strictly alone until new leaf growth begins before potting the new plants, but there may be less disruption if the cuttings are lifted and potted as soon as roots show. In either case, keep the potted cuttings in the same environment for two or three weeks more to let them acclimate to the pot, then gradually move them to increasingly bright situations.

Rooting time ranges from two weeks to three months—or more. The length of time depends primarily on the individual species, although good care on the part of the gardener can hasten the process. Since cold weather is likely to be in the offing after three months, cuttings that still look green and healthy should be moved into a similarly humid environment in the greenhouse, where they may root over the winter.

Bromeliads can be propagated by seeds or by division. Offsets that form around the base of the plant are carefully removed and planted in their own pots.

Layering

Propagation by layering is similar to rooting cuttings, but the part of the plant (usually a branch) to be rooted remains attached to the parent plant. Layering requires that one of the branches be low enough so that it can be bent into contact with the ground. Notch the point of contact and bury it in the ground. Securely immobilize it with a peg or a rock. A rock has the additional advantage of keeping the soil under it moist.

Layering is best done in spring. Root formation is likely to take several months. The most convenient technique may then be to leave the layer attached for a full year, for spring is also the best time for detaching it and growing it as a separate plant. Dig the branch from the ground at the point where roots have formed, then cut it from the parent plant below the roots and treat it as a rooted cutting.

A number of low-growing species will self-layer. Those can be treated in the same way.

The technique of air-layering can be used for some genera, such as *Dichorisandra* and *Dombeya*, that lack branches conveniently close to the ground. Wound the bark of a branch perhaps a foot from the end by cutting a shallow notch in it and wrap the branch completely with moistened sphagnum moss or a damp sponge. Cover the sponge over with tightly sealed plastic until roots begin to show through. Then detach the branch from the plant below the roots and treat the branch as a cutting.

Division

Most herbaceous plants, including tuberous species, can easily be increased by division. Take the plant from the ground and, depending on the species, either tease it apart into a number of smaller plants or slice it through the crown with a sharp knife or spade. Dormant plants need nothing more than a thorough watering once they have been replanted, while those which are evergreen or are already in active growth will do better with a week in humid, shaded conditions. The best time to divide most plants is just before the new growth starts (or perhaps when the new stems are just visible). The later in the growing season a plant is divided, the more aftercare it will need and the greater the chance of failure.

Grafting

More technically demanding than the other propagation techniques, grafting is best learned through example. It involves taking a cutting, or scion, of one cultivar and inserting it into the branch or stem of another (the stock), which is growing on its own roots. Usually the stock must be of the same genus as the scion, though in exceptional cases there is only a family connection. All of the leaves of the stock and scion are removed, as well as unused branches. In one simple type of graft, the chosen stock (which should be close in diameter to the scion) is split, and the scion is shaped into a wedge with some of the inner, living tissue (the cambium) remaining at the edges. The scion is inserted into the split, and the union is sealed with grafting wax.

POTS OR NOT?

There are two general ways that plants can be grown in a greenhouse; in containers or planted directly in the ground. The choice depends on the goals of the gardener and the requirements of the plants. Essentially all of the plants included in this book will succeed either way.

In the Ground

In-ground growing offers ease of culture and the possibility of integrated garden design,

Top: A cutting of one cactus is grafted onto the stem of another. A rubber band holds the cutting, or scion, in place.
Bottom: Plants grown in the ground rather than in pots require less frequent watering and in general are easier to care for.

which is to say that the plants can be grown close enough together to enhance one another through flower color, foliage pattern, or shape. Plants grown in the ground require much less frequent watering than those in pots, and they are much less vulnerable to sudden drought stress if watering is delayed. Problems with drainage, feeding, and the buildup of salts are less likely to occur. In general, plants in the ground are healthier and therefore better looking and more resistant to pests and cold. They also have more vigorous growth, which is not always desirable.

Before choosing to plant in the ground, consider what will happen inside the greenhouse over the summer. Will the atmosphere be too hot and dry for the species you want to endure? Some plants, including most camellias, many "eucalypts" (nursery slang for the *group* of eucalyptus species), and the proteas will survive and even prosper. In general, those species with thick and tough leaves do well inside in summer. If the species you want to grow need more moisture and cooler temperatures, consider designing a greenhouse from which most or all of the overhead glazing can be removed for the summer.

In Pots

Plants in pots can easily be moved around or out of the greenhouse, and are therefore easier to display at flowering time than plants in the ground. Intimately connected groupings are not as easy to set up, but nonetheless it is possible to put together very effective arrangements. If potted plants are to be moved from the greenhouse, however, certain points should be kept in mind.

Greenhouse plants in general require the bright, humid conditions that they find in the greenhouse and most definitely do not find in the house itself. Low light levels generally are not a problem, given that many of the plants, including those that flower in winter, are likely to be in a dormant or semidormant state (particularly if the greenhouse is a cool one), but the low humidity of the house will be a problem whether the plants are dormant or not. Nonetheless, almost all greenhouse plants can make the transition, as long as the stay in the house is limited.

Some genera, such as *Eucalyptus* and *Protea*, are terribly touchy and should spend no more than three or four days in the house. *Camellia* does much better, which is fortunate since its fall or winter blooms are so well received. Still, a week is long enough; longer, and it may start dropping buds before they open. With rosemary (*Rosmarinus officinalis*) the stint can be stretched to two weeks (a well-trained bush can make an interesting and unusual Christmas tree). One of the best of the woody species is sweetolive, *Osmanthus fragrans*. After three weeks it may look a little dusty and webby and may have lost the full force of its fragrance, but its vitality will be unaffected, and after two or three weeks of rest in the greenhouse it is ready to go again.

It is not a good idea to grow plants in pots in a subfreezing greenhouse because the roots are vulnerable to frost damage. Moving such plants into the house would not be feasible anyway, since the change in atmosphere would disrupt their hardened-off state, leaving them vulnerable to frost damage (ranging from blackening of new growth to the death of the whole plant) if they were returned to the greenhouse.

A major advantage of growing in pots, one that benefits the plants themselves, is that they can be taken outdoors, away from the heat and dryness of the greenhouse, for the summer. Such a move also exposes them to natural precipitation and local beneficial insects. In general, however, container growing is harder on plants than ground growing.

There is a perennial debate over the advantages and disadvantages of clay pots over plastic ones. Clay pots are porous and, therefore, permit the growing medium to dry out more quickly. Also, they often have a greater aesthetic appeal. Plastic pots reduce the frequency at which plants need watering, and they are light and cheap. Most plants will flourish in either clay or plastic pots. A clay pot is the better choice if a plant is to be plunged into the ground, pot and all; the porosity of the pot may help the plant to absorb moisture from the surrounding soil.

Other types of containers, such as troughs and window boxes, permit the growing of small plants in close harmony and yet may be as portable as individual pots. Plants grown in such containers tend to be intermediate in watering demands.

Opposite: Plants grown in pots have the advantage of being portable. They can be rearranged into varying displays at different seasons or as the gardener's mood dictates.

Plant Directory

All the plants in this directory have something special to contribute to a home greenhouse. Many bear colorful flowers in winter. Some provide fruit, or herbs, or fragrance to perfume the air. The selection is up to you.

The range of potential greenhouse plants is enormous, and this directory lists only a few hundred of the many thousands available. An attempt has been made to list at least a few plants from each of the categories discussed below.

Most of the common houseplants have been avoided; if you are interested in learning more about them, see Ortho's books *All About Houseplants* and *African Violets & Flowering Houseplants*. Some of the plants described, such as camellia and citrus, are commonly grown outdoors in mild regions but make excellent greenhouse plants for gardeners not fortunate enough to be able to grow them in the garden.

In general the plants that have been chosen are excellent greenhouse subjects. All are rewarding to grow. Some bear beautiful flowers or edible fruit; others are graceful, or unusual, or even bizarre.

All the plants in this directory are listed alphabetically by their scientific names. The "Directory of Common Names" on page 106 will help you to locate plants in the "Plant Directory" when you know only their common names.

Certain plants that share basic characteristics and needs are grouped together and listed under general category names such as *Annuals, Bromeliads, Gesneriads, Orchids,* and *Succulents.* Cross-referenced entries by individual plant names will lead you to the proper group listings.

The great majority of plants in this directory will do well if cared for with the standard culture techniques described in the second chapter. Any special needs are discussed in individual plant listings.

Bromeliads and orchids have similar environmental needs and thus grow well side by side. Here they are grouped close together to form the centerpiece of an impressive display.

Abutilon megapotamicum

Agapanthus orientalis

Abutilon
Flowering-maple

Family *Malvaceae*. Native to South America. Evergreen. Grows to 10 feet. A fast, even rank-growing shrub of loose habit grown for its odd, showy, drooping bell flowers. It is good for quick effect but also makes an impressive specimen plant. Begins flowering when small; size can be controlled to some extent by pruning and in particular by pinching back the growing tips. Standard culture with moist soil and some shading in summer. Susceptible to whiteflies and scale. Because cuttings root so readily, it is often best to keep a plant going with new cuttings and discard the parent plant when it becomes too large.

A. *hybridum* (*A. globosum*) Characterized by arching, upright growth and broad, maplelike leaves. Flowers in shades of orange, red, white, and yellow are borne primarily April to June but also appear sporadically in other seasons. Plants with white and yellow flowers are particularly long

blooming. Tolerant of cool conditions, down to 32° F. 'Apricot Belle' bears coral pink flowers; 'Ashford Red', crimson; 'Clementine', orange and red; 'Silver Belle', white.

A. *megapotamicum* Somewhat lax and vinelike in growth. Yellow flowers emerge from a crimson calyx, primarily May to September. The yellow-mottled leaves of variety 'Variegata' go especially well with the flowers. Can tolerate some frost, to about 25° F.

Achimenes hybrids
Magicflower

See *Gesneriads*

Adenium
See *Succulents*

Adiantum
See *Ferns*

Aechmea
See *Bromeliads*

Aeonium
See *Succulents*

Aeschynanthus obconicus
Lipstick-plant

See *Gesneriads*

Agapanthus
African-lily, lily-of-the-Nile

Family *Amaryllidaceae*. Native to South Africa. Evergreen and deciduous perennials. *Agapanthus* has thick, fleshy roots and straplike, arching leaves, above which rise umbels of blue or occasionally white flowers in summer. This well-shaped plant is suitable for a formal arrangement. It is usually grown in a pot; the roots may, however, crack the pot in time unless the plant is frequently divided. It is easy to grow, requiring standard treatment during the growing

season and, for those that go dormant, an almost complete withholding of water during winter. Propagation is by seed or division; division is best done as growth starts in the spring. Seed can be sown at any time, but seedlings are easier to handle and come along more vigorously in warmer weather. Three years to flowering size from seed.

A. *campanulatus* Similar to *A. africanus* and *A. umbellatus*. Deciduous. Grows to 2½ feet. Good for bedding out in summer and storing under the greenhouse benches in winter. Begin watering when growth becomes visible in spring; withhold water when leaves turn yellow in fall.

A. *praecox* Includes subspecies *minimus, orientalis* (white and blue forms), and *praecox*. Listed also as *A. orientalis*. Evergreen. Grows to 2½ to 3 feet, depending on subspecies (*minimus* is the smallest). Vigorous. Needs some water in winter.

Allamanda cathartica

Browallia speciosa

Allamanda

Family *Apocynaceae*. Native to tropical South America. Evergreen.

A. cathartica (golden trumpet vine) The most commonly grown species. Grows to 15 feet. A vigorous climber that bears large, flaring, golden yellow flowers in spring and summer. Spectacular if it can be grown in the ground and trained up the south-facing wall of the greenhouse. It does well in a pot for a time but tends to outgrow it; it can stay longer in the pot if pruned. Standard culture. Minimum temperature 50° F. Susceptible to mealybugs. Propagate by cuttings.

Aloe

See *Succulents*

Ananas comosus

See *Bromeliads*

Annuals

In the strict sense, annuals are plant species that germinate, flower, set seed, and die in the course of a single growing season. However, when the term is applied to the plants grown in a greenhouse, it can also refer to perennials that are customarily kept for only a single season of flowering. *Primula obconica*, for instance, will come back the second season, but will definitely be inferior to the first season in size, vigor, and quantity of flowers. The plants described as annuals in this book provide quick bloom for one season. After that they should probably be discarded, although this does not rule out experimentation.

The annuals chosen for inclusion share another characteristic—they are all easy to grow. They require standard soil, watering, and feeding and, if started from seed, are quick to germinate and easy to handle as seedlings. They differ in the seasons in which they normally bloom, but the emphasis in

a greenhouse is usually on achieving flowers in fall and winter. That can mean digging up long-flowering plants from the summer garden and bringing them inside, or choosing the rather few species that flower in fall or winter. Sowing later than normal can also delay flowering until the desired season, but this technique won't work if bud formation is photoperiod dependent (requiring a specific length of daylight) unless supplemental light is provided.

Antirrhinum majus
Snapdragon

Grows to 8 to 30 inches. One of the most reliable annuals for greenhouse growing and winter bloom. Successive sowings will provide waves of flowers from December to March, with each wave lasting 1½ to 2 months. Sow in mid-July for mid-December bloom, or dig up plants in full bloom in the garden before severe frost strikes. Good in a cool, even cold greenhouse.

Browallia speciosa

Evergreen, bushy perennial, though often treated as an annual. Grows to 2 feet, less in the dwarf varieties. Interesting felted foliage. Blue or white flowers, in summer from an early spring sowing, in winter if sown in the fall. Needs warmth (55° F minimum), good light, standard soil, and frequent feeding with dilute fertilizer. Can be propagated by cuttings; plants are usually acquired, however, through seeds. Can be kept going by severe cutting back in the fall, although the resulting plant tends to become leggier and less attractive than a new plant raised from a cutting. Often grown in hanging pots.

Calceolaria crenatiflora

Grows to 12 inches. A short-lived perennial that deteriorates after the first season of bloom. Bears spectacular slipper flowers in a wide range of colors, usually bicolors. Sow in heat (60° F is the best germination temperature);

Annuals

The greenhouse has just been finished and winter is on the way. What can be done to start the season off with a splash of color? Annuals!

Annuals are fast-off-the-mark plants, designed by nature to throw all possible energy into the business of reproduction, which translates into flowering early and flowering often. Most annuals expend their energy most profligately during summer, when pollinators are also around in abundance, but there are some species that naturally bloom late in the season. Many of the all-summer bloomers will push on into fall and early winter, as long as there is warmth to spur them on.

Even with a more mature, well-stocked greenhouse, there is a strong temptation to fill it up further as fall approaches and annuals in the outside garden reach their peak. What a shame to see such perfection cut down by the first killing frost! Dug up and potted, they can be brought inside for another two months.

In summer, annuals can lighten up a greenhouse that is largely filled with winter-blooming perennial plants. That greenhouse will need to be well ventilated, but if the perennials are to remain inside that is necessary anyway. The annuals must be heat resistant, and they must be carefully watered and fed, but given that care they will make the summer greenhouse as glowing as the garden outside.

Nemesia strumosa

Chrysanthemum vestitum

Chrysanthemum frutescens

grow cool (50° F night temperature suits them best, preferably with a rise of no more than 10 degrees or so during the day). Allow 4 to 9 months, depending on variety, from sowing to flowering.

Calendula officinalis

Also called pot-marigold. Grows to 18 inches. An excellent annual for the cooler greenhouse, since it prefers temperatures below 45° F. Large orange or yellow flowers begin to appear 2½ months after sowing; sow in July for flowers from October to January.

Chrysanthemum

Chrysanthemum

Family *Compositae*. Grows to 2 feet. Familiar and valuable garden plants that include two species that bring fall and winter color to the greenhouse. Although perennial, they are generally used as annuals, with cuttings being taken from the parent plant each summer to replace the parent as it becomes too large and gangly. Easily grown under standard culture.

C. × morifolium (*C. vestitum*) Florist's chrysanthemum; hybrid origin. Woody-stemmed and wide spreading, with large, lobed leaves. Flowers occur in a wide range of reds, pinks, oranges, and purples, as well as white, with flower shape being just as variable. Blooms from late summer to winter. Can endure some frost but flowers best and longest with a minimum temperature of 40° F; prefers cool conditions.

C. frutescens (Marguerite) Native to Canary Islands. A more refined but less hardy plant, damaged by frost. Finely divided leaves; large flowers with yellow centers and white rays; rays can also be yellow or pink in hybrids with *C. coronopifolium*.

Dianthus caryophyllus
Carnation

Grows to 8 inches. Perennial that doesn't improve with age, but can be kept going with cuttings. Blooms in 5 months from seed; heaviest bloom is in summer but continues through winter. The Knight series does well in a home greenhouse, bearing the typical large, double carnation flowers in shades of red, pink, and white. The leaves suggest broadened grass stems and are an attractive gray-green. Needs a fairly steady temperature level of 45° to 50° F.

Matthiola incana
Stock

An annual well suited to the greenhouse; thrives in cool conditions. Fragrant red, pink, or white flowers are borne 9 to 12 weeks after sowing, depending on variety. Upright growth reaches 15 to 20 inches. Matte green leaves are modestly attractive. Standard culture.

Nemesia species

Family *Scrophulariaceae*. Native to South Africa. Grows to 10 inches. A bushy annual with abundant flowers in many bright colors. Sow in early September for flowers through the winter.

Petunia species

Family *Solanaceae*. Native to tropical South America. Grows to 20 inches. Large, funnel-shaped flowers in a wide range of colors liberally cover the mounded plants all summer long. The lax, succulent stems are easily broken, but growth is rapid, quickly filling in the scars. As with marigolds, petunias are still going strong when overcome by frost. They are easily moved inside—most easily if already growing in a pot. They can also be readily dug up if in the ground or, if the plant has grown straggly, can be transferred by cuttings. The plants should be severely cut back in any case, and with the new growth will come a new flush of bloom. Feed regularly at this time.

Primula malacoides

Nasturtium 'Monet'

Primula

Family *Primulaceae.* Grows to 15 inches. These plants bloom naturally in winter, and are ideally suited to the moist environment of the cold greenhouse; they flower sturdily in the face of temperatures of freezing and somewhat below. *P. malacoides* is a true annual. Native to China. It has umbels of flowers in pinks, purples, and white held well above the foliage. Sow seed in April. *P. obconica,* also native to China, has perennial tendencies and may be stretched to a second season, but it is in general more rewarding to start anew from seed each year. Flowers are large and bright, in unusual shades of red, pink, purple, and white. Some people have an allergic reaction to the leaves. Start seed in January and feed plants heavily during the summer.

Salvia splendens

Grows to 20 inches. The screaming red salvia that seems a cliché by the end of the summer will take on new meaning if moved into the greenhouse to continue its flowering. It is readily dug up and potted, without needing to be cut back, or it can be propagated by rooting cuttings of basal growth.

Senecio cruentus
Cineraria

Grows to 12 to 24 inches. A colorful annual with bright, glowing daisy flowers in unusual shades of pink, red, purple and blue, as well as white, often with contrasting bands. Leaves are large and felted. It can readily be grown for winter bloom, with seed

sown in May for a December flowering. Grow moist and cool, 45° to 50° F.

Tagetes erecta
Marigold

Grows to 6 to 30 inches. Marigolds in the outside garden build up steam as the temperature drops in the fall, only to be cut down by frost at their peak. The clumps can in fact be dug up readily and brought into the greenhouse, where they will bloom for many weeks more. Alternatively, seeds can be sown in August and the seedlings kept in pots. There are many dwarf varieties to choose from; among the best are the *T. tenuifolia* cultivars.

Tropaeolum species
Nasturtium

Family *Tropaeolaceae.* Native to tropical America. Grows to 8 inches. Excellent spreading, trailing annual with yellow or orange flowers. Best in cool temperatures. Leaves and flowers are good in a salad, but its susceptibility to aphids may require spraying. Four months from seed to flowering.

Viola
Violet

Grows to 6 to 10 inches. Pansies and johnny-jump-ups, both of which are members of this genus, come into their own with the arrival of cool weather, quickening into growth and even putting out one or a few blooms right up to hard frost. Garden plants can be dug up and brought into the greenhouse, where they will flower more abundantly for several weeks longer. *V. odorata* (sweet violet) is a true perennial that will bloom in December if

Ardisia crispa

Azalea hybrid

given the protection of even the coldest greenhouse. It is delightfully fragrant but quite untidy, and is probably best treated as a temporary resident, as are the other violets.

Zinnia species

Family *Compositae*. Native to Mexico. Dwarf zinnia varieties, which grow to no more than 18 to 24 inches, make pleasant container plants for the greenhouse in the fall. They will not be as profusely covered with flowers as they were outside during the summer. Sow seeds in early June.

Antirrhinum majus
Snapdragon

See *Annuals*

Aphelandra

Family *Acanthaceae*. Native to tropical America. Evergreen shrub of bold appearance. Most commonly grown, and boldest, is the following:

A. squarrosa (zebraplant) Grows to 4 feet. Vividly striped leaves have earned this species its common name; under favorable conditions they will be topped by yellow spires of tubular flowers and their surrounding bracts. Blooms late summer to early winter. Easily grown and well known as a houseplant. In the greenhouse it needs warmth (greater than 45° F) and shading from the noon sun; otherwise standard culture. Prune after flowering to prevent legginess. Propagate by cuttings in spring or early summer, or by seeds. 'Louisae', the cultivar most readily available, is compact with relatively small leaves; more recent cultivars such as 'Apollo White' and 'Dania' are even more compact and have more pronounced leaf veining.

Aporocactus flagelliformis

See *Cactaceae*

Ardisia

Family *Myrsinaceae*. Evergreen shrubs, only one of which is commonly grown in the greenhouse:

A. crispa (A. crenata; A. crenulata) (coralberry) Native to Southeast Asia. Grows to 4 feet. Not an exciting plant, but serviceable and obliging, and in a quiet way very ornamental. Primarily grown for the glossy foliage and the bright red berries that appear in fall and last through the winter. The tiny white flowers that precede the berries are somewhat fragrant. Good, single-stemmed habit; a cheery specimen plant in the greenhouse. Standard culture; tolerates drought and low light levels during winter when dormant. Grows fairly slowly and blooms when small (10 inches); readily pruned and shaped. Susceptible to scale. Propagate by cuttings or seed; the berries may self-sow about the base of the plant.

Asplenium nidus

See *Ferns*

Astrophytum asterias

See *Cactaceae*

Azalea

Family *Ericaceae*. Native to southern China and India. Evergreen and deciduous shrubs, members of the genus *Rhododendron* but distinctive enough to be considered separately. There are many types of azaleas, but the most valuable for the greenhouse are those evergreen varieties that bloom in winter. By and large these are the Belgian Indicas, a group that was bred for greenhouse growing. They are relatively tender. They survive to 20° F, but to bloom in winter they need warmer conditions, 35° F or above. They begin blooming when about 1 foot high; mature height is 2 to 3 feet.

Begonia listada

Babiana stricta

Begonia masoniana

Azaleas in general are better greenhouse plants than rhododendrons because they are more tolerant of heat, but that is far from saying they are ideally suited. They are best moved outdoors for the summer, since they are quite susceptible to fungal diseases brought on by the indoor combination of heat and humidity. They require shading from direct summer sunlight. Their growing medium must be acid and high in organic matter, both of which requirements can be met by increasing the amount of peat in the medium. A medium that is not acid enough will result in chlorosis, a yellowing of the leaves. Frequent feeding is needed during the growing season; use a fertilizer designed for acid-loving plants. Water enough to keep the medium moist but not wet.

The following cultivars bloom from October to March or April. Double, semidouble, and single refer to the number of petals that make up the flower, with a double having approximately twice as many

flowers as a single, and a semidouble somewhere in between.

'Albert and Elizabeth': flowers double; white with pink edges. One of the most commonly available, often sold at nurseries.

'Avenir': flowers double; coppery pink.

'California Sunset': flowers single; pink-edged white.

'Chimes': flowers semidouble; red; bell-shaped.

'Mme. Alfred Sanders': compact; flowers double; red.

'Orange Sanders': as above, but orange.

'Perle de Swynaerde': flowers double; white.

'Red Poppy': flowers single to semidouble; red.

Babiana
Baboonflower

Family *Iridaceae*. Native to South Africa. Summer-dormant; bulbous. Notable for bright flowers, large for the size of the plant, borne in early spring. The sword-shaped leaves are also attractive; even when turning brown they are not an eyesore,

though they should be removed as soon as they are thoroughly brown. Good container plant. Standard culture, except that watering and feeding requirements are greatest in winter, the reverse of the usual pattern. Not oversensitive to water in summer if the soil is well drained. May be attacked by spider mites, particularly as spring advances. Easily grown from seed; requires two years or so to reach flowering size. Bulbs multiply rapidly and can be divided when dormant. Hardy to 20° to 25° F. Most widely available as hybrids in shades of blue, mauve, and purple.

B. pulchra Grows to 12 inches. Flowers are blue marked with wine red.

B. pygmaea Grows to 6 inches. Valuable for its small size and its large flowers, which are yellow with purple centers.

B. stricta Grows to 4 inches. Dark pink flowers. *B. stricta* 'Rubrocyanea', often listed as *B. rubrocyanea*, is somewhat larger at 6 inches and has striking blue flowers with red centers.

Begonia
Begonia

Family *Begoniaceae*. Native to Old and New World tropics and temperate Asia. Evergreen and deciduous herbaceous perennials, with some tuberous species.

The begonia is the quintessential houseplant. It is widely popular, partly because it is so adaptable to the indoor environment and partly because it is so attractive. Its beauty makes it worth growing in the greenhouse as well. The begonias suitable for greenhouse growing are the semituberous, fibrous-rooted, rhizomatous, and Rex varieties. There are other types, such as tuberous and semperflorens, that flower in summer and have no need of a greenhouse. Riegers, which bloom in winter, are spectacular, but they are difficult to grow because they are very susceptible to mildew.

Most begonias are evergreen, herbaceous plants, though a few have a dormant

Begonia coccinea

Begonia 'Fireworks'

period. All are grown for their distinctively asymmetric foliage; in some the flowers are insignificant, in others, outstanding.

Culture in most cases is straightforward. Soil should be lighter than standard, watering and feeding copious in the growing season, though the rhizomatous types are amazingly drought tolerant. The tiny seedlings are somewhat difficult to handle.

The major cultural variables are light and warmth. All species need some shading from the summer sun, but the degree needed varies. Semituberous begonias need the least shade; fibrous-rooted and rhizomatous need more; and Rex should receive no direct sun at all. In any case, all begonias do much better if moved to a shady spot outdoors for the summer.

The need for warmth varies as well. The Rex requires a minimum temperature of 60° F. For fibrous-rooted and rhizomatous begonias, 50° F is minimum. At least one semituberous begonia can take a minimum temperature of 12° F, during dormancy.

Fibrous-rooted begonias

This is an enormous group, ranging from species that grow to only 4 inches tall and need the high humidity of a terrarium to cane-stem species that grow to 12 feet and can fill a greenhouse with their flowers. Most are sturdy and amenable, requiring only the general culture outlined above. *B. coccinea* (angel-wing) is a tall-growing cane-stem species with constant umbels of coral red flowers. *B. dichroa* is low and glossy-leaved with brilliant orange and white flowers. *B. listada* is grown mostly for its velvety, arrow-shaped leaves, but it also bears cream-colored flowers in autumn. Propagate by seed, cuttings of the canes, and division.

Rex begonias

These have the most colorful foliage of all, and in many cases have showy flowers as well. They are relatively unsuited to greenhouse growing but will do well in a warm,

moist greenhouse if kept in a shady spot, such as under the growing benches. There are many distinct kinds. Among the most popular are 'Fireworks', with wine red veins on a silver background; *B. masoniana* (iron-cross), with its chocolate brown cross on an apple green background; and 'Painted Lady', an artist's palette of red and green. Propagate by division. They can also be propagated by seed, but selected forms may not come true.

Rhizomatous begonias

These are distinguished by their thick, succulent stems that can wander and sprawl. In general they are grown more for foliage than for flowers. They are drought and shade tolerant, but for the most satisfactory results, they should be given a good deal of indirect light when growing in the summer. *B. caroliniifolia* is one of the tallest and toughest, growing to 2 feet high with large, palmate leaves and sprays of small white flowers in late winter. *B. goegoensis* has attractive bronzy leaves with spiderlike webbing; it

bears pink flowers in winter. 'Othello' is a compact grower with clustered, curled, black-green leaves and white flowers in spring, held well above the foliage. Propagate by seed and by cutting up the stems and inserting the pieces in moist sand, best done in summer.

Semituberous begonias

Like the fully tuberous species, these begonias bloom in the summer and are dormant in winter. One, *B. sutherlandii*, is attractive, small, and hardy (to 12° F), and thus well suited for growing in the ground in a subfreezing greenhouse. It has orange flowers from July to October, grows to 8 inches high with a spread of 12 inches, and likes a lot of moisture when growing. Propagate by seed and by division when dormant.

Billbergia nutans

See *Bromeliads*

Blechnum gibbum

See *Ferns*

Bougainvillea 'Orange Fiesta'

Bougainvillea 'Pink Pixie'

Bougainvillea hybrid

Bougainvillea

Bougainvillea

Family *Nyctaginaceae*. Native to South America. Evergreen vining shrubs. Can grow to 20 feet, although some varieties are much smaller. Bougainvillea bears large, showy bracts that surround the tiny flowers in fall and winter. It is a standard item in gardens in the tropics and the Gulf Coast states and southern California; the vigorous growth seen there would seem to exclude it from greenhouse growing, but in fact it can easily be kept to size by pruning. Possible in a pot but much better in the ground, perhaps trained up the north wall of the greenhouse. Standard light and soil. Feed in spring and early summer. Water frequently at feeding time, but much less in midsummer, even to the point of allowing slight wilting, to induce flowering. Plants that are to be transferred from a container must be handled carefully because the roots do not form a solid ball. Grows

best at a minimum temperature greater than 50° F, but can endure considerable frost. Mature plants can go down to 25° F or lower. Susceptible to mealybugs. Propagate by cuttings in summer. Can also be raised from seed but will almost certainly be inferior, with thorns enlarged and bracts reduced.

There are several species, but named hybrids (mostly crosses of *B. glabra* and *B. peruviana*) are the most generally grown. Good, clear colors, particularly yellows, in unnamed cultivars may also be available locally. Here are some good modern ones:

'Barbara Karst': red flowers; blooms readily and profusely.

'Betty Hendry': red flowers; long blooming period; begins flowering when young.

'Double Gold': double, golden orange flowers. Double pink, red, and white are also available.

'Pink Pixie': pink flowers; miniature.

'Temple Fire': bronze red flowers. More shrublike in growth; small.

Brachycome

Family *Compositae*. Native to Australia. Best known for *B. iberidifolia*, the Swan River daisy, a choice summer-blooming annual. For the greenhouse, however, there is one equally choice evergreen perennial:

B. multiflora (creeping subshrub)   Grows to 8 inches. The specific name tells it all—this plant is constantly spangled with light blue flowers. It is also in other ways well-nigh the perfect greenhouse plant. It has attractive, tidy needle leaves; no special demand for feeding or soil, beyond good drainage; and an impressive drought tolerance for a non-succulent. Does best in full sun. Can be pruned readily but is well-mannered without it. Frost tolerance unknown but is untouched at 32° F. Propagate by cuttings or layers; it does not readily self-layer, so the gardener must intervene. Good for hanging baskets.

Bromeliads

Family *Bromeliaceae*. Native to the Americas. Evergreen herbaceous plants in a number of genera distinguished, in most cases, by a cuplike arrangement of the leaves, an epiphytic habit, and extreme durability. The thick, straplike leaves come in many colors and designs. Odd and colorful flowers are borne by some species. At least one species, *Ananas comosus*, the pineapple, bears edible fruit. Because of their toughness and distinctive appearance, bromeliads make excellent container plants. They are so distinctive, however, that they can be difficult to blend with more conventional plants.

Grow in full sun in light, rapidly draining, highly organic soil. The epiphytic species can be grown in an orchid mix. Keep well watered in

Bromeliads

Similar environmental challenges often lead to convergent evolution, but not in the case of bromeliads and orchids. These two large groups of tree-dwelling plants share the same epiphytic environment and make their livings from the same chance depositions of organic debris. To make the most of its limited water supply, the orchid folds its leaves in, conserving whatever water its thick roots can absorb. Taking the opposite approach, the bromeliad opens its leaves wide to accumulate what it can in their embrace, that often being enough water to serve as a hatching pond for tree-frog tadpoles.

Bromeliads are in general easier to grow than orchids, being less fussy about drainage and the composition of the growing medium. They do have their disadvantages, of course. Chief among them is that many have large, aggressively toothed leaves that constitute a distinct hazard to passersby. They also, like ferns, have a somewhat static quality, most evident in those that are grown primarily for foliage. They sit there, looking good but not doing much beyond slowly producing offsets. That itself is a valuable function, however, given the spectacular foliage of some varieties.

Bromeliads are among the most desirable greenhouse plants—tough, distinctive, always attractive in foliage, and sometimes uniquely lovely in flower.

Guzmania lingulata and *Vriesia* species

Billbergia nutans

Brunfelsia americana

summer (filling the cup in those species that have one) and feed frequently with dilute fertilizer. Water sparingly in winter. Best in a warm greenhouse; minimum temperature 55° to 60° F. Propagate in spring by potting up the offsets that form around the base of the plant, treating them as cuttings, or by seeds; allow 4 to 5 years to reach flowering size.

Aechmea
'Foster's Favorite'

Has an exaggerated vase shape formed by wine red, shiny leaves, 1 foot or more long. Flowers are coral red and blue, and striking; they may be followed by brilliant red berries. *A. fasciata*, from Brazil, grows to 20 inches high. It is grown as much for its brightly marked foliage as for its flowers. Flowers are dark blue, surrounded by pink bracts. *A. lueddemanniana*, another favorite, can grow as tall as 30 inches, and almost as broad. Its flowers are initially blue, turning to red as they age. It is from Central America.

Ananas comosus

The pineapple is worth growing, but there are caveats—it is large, up to 3 feet at flowering size, and the long leaves are painfully jagged. It is readily available, however; the leafy top of a pineapple forms roots if detached and placed in a warm enclosure. It requires a more loamy medium than most bromeliads.

Billbergia nutans

Grows to 16 inches. A floriferous species; in early spring it bears greenish yellow flowers with purple-blue margins, set off by pink bracts. A vigorous grower; rosettes of dark green leaves quickly form sizable clumps.

Guzmania

Similar to *Aechmea* in appearance. There is so much confusion in nomenclature that plants are often simply described as *Guzmania* species or hybrids. One well-known species is *G. sanguinea*, a native of Central and South America. Grows to 12 inches.

Inner leaves are bright red blotched with yellow; outer, older leaves are dull green. Small, yellowish flowers are of less significance than the foliage.

Tillandsia cyanea

Grows to 12 inches. Forms a large clump of rosettes in time. Striking, showy inflorescence combining a deep-pink bract and violet-blue flowers, one or two opening sequentially over a long period.

Vriesea hieroglyphica

Grows to 1½ feet. Has purple-brown leaves so intricately marked with brownish green as to suggest writing. A striking foliage plant, it can also produce dull yellow flowers borne on a 3-foot stalk. Other *Vriesea* species, not well identified but readily available, have much brighter, showier flowers.

Browallia

See *Annuals*

Brunfelsia

Family *Solanaceae*. Native to tropical America. Evergreen shrubs that have large, flat flowers with crinkled margins. Stately container plants. Tip pruning is desirable to keep the plants in good form. Standard culture with extra humidity, some shading from summer sun, and an acid soil. Propagate by cuttings.

B. americana (lady-of-the-night) Grows to 10 feet. Long, yellow, night-fragrant flowers, which fade to white with age, are borne in June. Minimum temperature 50° F.

B. calycina and *B. paucifolia* (yesterday-today-and-tomorrow) Grows to 4 feet. So called because the flowers go through a dramatic change with age, opening blue-violet and fading to white in 3 days or so. An excellent container plant, of slow growth and good form if pruned; blooms winter into summer. Best at a minimum temperature of 50° F but will hold its own at 45° F if kept dry. At lower temperatures it will show its displeasure by losing its leaves, but will recover.

Brunfelsia calycina

Hyacinthus orientalis

Bulbs for Forcing

There is a vast array of bulbous plants, including corms, rhizomes, and tubers as well as true bulbs. Those considered here fall into one specific subset, the familiar hardy spring bulbs that need a period of cold to initiate bud formation and flowering: crocus, daffodil, grapehyacinth, hyacinth, scilla, snowdrop, and tulip. Their general culture is the same: bright light and abundant fertilizer and water when in growth. Active growth is followed by a complete withdrawal from the aboveground world. At that stage they are impervious to dryness and heat (barring direct sunlight on an exposed pot) and can tolerate normal summer moisture as long as the growing medium is well drained.

These plants offer a way of enjoying the pleasures of spring early and in comfort. They can bring intense splashes of color to the greenhouse in February and March—or later, if desired, but then they are in competition with those outside. The greenhouse has two advantages over the house as a growing environment: The period of bloom is much longer in a greenhouse (a week is typically the extreme limit in the house, versus two weeks or so in a cool greenhouse) and the bulbs have some hope of a future life, being able to rebuild their energy supplies there through photosynthesis once the leaves appear.

The routine for forcing bulbs is simple: First, chill the bulbs for 6 to 8 weeks, or buy prechilled ones. The bulbs need moisture as well as coolness, so they should be in pots during this period, with the medium slightly moist. Experience indicates that sufficient chilling will occur if the temperature remains below about 45° F. There is no clear-cut lower limit since these species can withstand hard freezes, but root and bud development tend to proceed more swiftly at a higher temperature.

Second, bring the bulbs into warmth. Roots or shoots will tell when. If roots show through the drainage hole or if shoots break through the soil, the plant is ready for active growth. Warmth can mean anything from 45° F on up; the whole life cycle is accelerated as the temperature goes up. The flowering time can be manipulated by increasing or decreasing the temperature as the buds are developing; bloom can then be prolonged by keeping the plant at the lowest temperature possible.

Crocus
Crocus

Any type of crocus responds well to forcing. In addition, a number of species naturally bloom in the winter, including *C. imperati, C. laevigatus,* and *C. ochroleucus,* although those are best in a subfreezing greenhouse if they are to be grown permanently. *C. vernus,* the familiar Dutch crocus in all its variety, is readily available and satisfying. *C. sieberi* and *C. tomasinianus* are smaller and tidier; they run to blues, violets, and whites. *C. ancyrensis* is a bright to brassy yellow and naturally very early.

Galanthus
Snowdrop

The downturned white flowers tipped with green are not showy but are pleasant and evocative of spring. Snowdrops are easy to force but not so easy to keep going in a pot, where they are vulnerable to drought stress. *G. elwesii* performs relatively well.

Hyacinthus
Hyacinth

Notable for the fullness, brightness, and fragrance of their spikes of flowers. Hyacinths are best mixed with

Bulbs for Forcing

Bulbs are enlarged storage organs, developed by some plants as a way of coping with the more extreme vagaries of nature. If local conditions don't suit it, a bulbous plant can escape into dormancy until they improve. This adaptation plays directly into the hands of the greenhouse gardener, who can manipulate the environment to bring on and break dormancy at any season.

There is an added advantage to such species: bulbs are usually available in flowering size. No waiting for rewards for one season or two—tulips or daffodils will burst into blossom the spring after they are planted. If grown well (as is easily done in a greenhouse) the bulbs will rapidly increase in size and number, providing an even greater abundance of bloom in succeeding years.

Although abundance of bloom is readily achieved, length of bloom is generally quite short. The gardener must therefore decide how much effort and space to commit to a brief but thoroughly glorious explosion of color.

Iris 'Dazzling Gold'

Forced bulbs in a vase

Crocus vernus

Iris reticulata

Narcissus hybrid

other plants rather than massed because of their stiff, almost artificial appearance. Varieties differ only in flower color; all are equally responsive.

Iris
Iris

The best of the bulbous irises for forcing are *I. histrioides* and *I. danfordiae*. The flowers of both are large and brilliant, the former royal blue with yellow markings, the latter clear yellow. The flowers stand out prominently before leaves appear. The leaves then rise to a foot or more. *I. danfordiae* has the awkward habit of splitting into myriad bulblets after flowering, each of which takes many years to reach flowering size. Both species need sun and a well-drained medium.

Muscari
Grapehyacinth

Very easygoing and tidy, in both blue and white forms. There are not many varieties to choose from, but *M. armeniacum* 'Cantab' is particularly free-flowering.

Narcissus
Daffodil

The paperwhite narcissus (*N. papyraceus*) is probably the plant that most often comes to mind when forcing is mentioned, yet it doesn't really need forcing at all since its natural time of bloom is fall and winter. However, it has the amiable habit of coming into flower at any season if the bulbs are given a sufficient period of dormancy and then kept moist. It can be grown in the greenhouse, but the foliage is long, lax, and not very attractive. The standard outdoor daffodils are good forcing subjects, offering a wide range of sizes, shapes, and colors. *N. asturiensis* at 4 inches is at the lower end of things; it bears a yellow trumpet flower. Among the standard sizes, 'King Alfred' (deep gold) and 'Hawera' (lemon yellow) are particularly dependable and rewarding. *N. bulbocodium*, in some of its forms, blooms in autumn and winter so is discussed separately (see page 86).

Scilla

The species *S. siberica* is low and vigorous with flowers of intense blue. *S. tubergeniana* has flowers of an undistinguished pinkish white, but it is very easy to force, since it requires a minimum of chilling and blooms very early.

Tulipa
Tulip

Tulips are colorful and showy wherever they are grown. They can put on a fine display in the greenhouse, but nonetheless they are not quite the naturals that some other genera are. They require a longer period of chilling (10 to 12 weeks) and are reluctant to bloom a lot earlier than their normal time outside. For earliest bloom, it is necessary to choose the types that are naturally early flowering, which in general are such species tulips as *T. batalinii* and *T. kaufmanniana*, but their flowers do not tend to last well. Darwin tulips are later but more enduring and are among the most satisfactory; any of the hybrid types are well worth trying.

Cactaceae
Cacti

An all-American family, though some species have become naturalized worldwide. They are divided here into two groups: Group 1 are the flat-leaved, spineless epiphytic cacti that require some shading and warm winter temperatures. Group 2 are the more typical spined, hardy sun lovers.

In either case, they fall into the category of succulents (see page 99) and fill the same ornamental niche. Like all succulents, they require very good drainage and greatly reduced watering in winter. The cacti are so large a group, however, with so many members readily available, they merit an entry of their own.

GROUP 1 CACTI

Although tree-dwellers like orchids or bromeliads, these do not have the same narrowly defined requirements for a

Epiphyllum ackermannii

Selenicereus hybrid

growing medium; they thrive in just about any type of soil. In general they are easy to grow if given shade and warmth. They are equally well suited to the house and the greenhouse, being just as tolerant of low humidity as any other cactus. They do need more watering than the group 2 species in winter, however, particularly in the drier atmosphere of a warmer greenhouse. They bear either enormous individual flowers or plant-covering masses of smaller ones.

Aporocactus flagelliformis
Rattail cactus

A hanging-basket cactus, with trailing stems up to 3 feet long that bear large red or pink flowers in spring.

Epiphyllum (Nopalxochia) ackermannii hybrids

Plants that can be sturdy, erect, and columnar or flat-leaved and arching, in general reaching as much as 3 feet in height. All bear large, fragrant blossoms, primarily in summer but also sporadically throughout the year.

'Autumn': pink flowers.
'Cambodia': red flowers.
'Paul de Longpre': yellow flowers.
'Queen of the Night': white flowers; a nocturnal bloomer.

Rhipsalis paradoxa
Chain cactus

Grows to 3 feet. Flat pads with narrow linking necks droop laxly; best in a hanging pot. White flowers are borne profusely at the tips of the branches in spring.

Schlumbergera bridgesii (Zygocactus)

Grows to 1½ feet. The familiar Christmas cactus. Flat, arching stems bear a dense mass of red, pink, or white flowers in December. *S. gaertneri* (Easter cactus) and *S. truncata* (Thanksgiving cactus) similarly adorn their respective holidays. Bud formation is initiated by length of daylight, so exposure to artificial light at the critical time of year can interfere with flower set. For this reason they are good plants for a greenhouse.

Selenicereus grandiflorus
Nightblooming cereus

Grows to 16 feet. An almost impossibly gawky and awkward plant, nonetheless forgiven for its memorable flowers, which are immense, white, and fragrant. Each flower lasts only a single night. Blooming time is primarily in spring and fall. Sparse, vinelike growth can be more or less satisfactorily dealt with by interweaving it with a sturdier, treelike plant.

GROUP 2 CACTI

These are desert cacti with water-conserving globose shapes or thick, fleshy pads, usually well armed with spines or dense hair. Although some species reach treelike dimensions, those considered here are naturally limited in size, growing to no more than 3 feet after many years and flowering when much smaller. These species are the true sun lovers—they will not do well without it in the summer. In winter they are dormant and

fairly indifferent to light level. Given the right conditions, they are ready bloomers, bearing outsized, vividly colored flowers in late spring or early summer. They are among the choicest of plants for container gardens, and they blend well with other types of plants that also have restrained, well-defined growth.

The globular kinds produce pups (miniatures of themselves that appear as swellings around the base) that can be detached and treated as cuttings. These plants tend to have a fair degree of hardiness and are well worth trying in a subfreezing greenhouse.

Astrophytum asterias
Sand-dollar

Native to Mexico and southern Texas. A 3-inch-wide flattened globe, armed with nothing more than wooly areoles (tufts). Yellow flowers come from the very top of the plant. *A. myriostigma* (bishop's-cap) grows to 2 feet. Its segments are well-defined, its surface leathery in appearance, its flowers yellow.

Cacti

Although the term *cactus* tends to call up an image of a distinctive, coherent, and unique plant group, in fact cacti occur in a wide variety of forms and are painstakingly imitated by members of other families. Almost all cacti share a common adaptation to drought: they have dispensed with leaves and rely instead on thick, water-conserving stems for photosynthesis. The stems may be elongate or globular, one or many.

Most cacti produce large or very large flowers, up to 6 inches across in some species. Thus, though they are commonly considered foliage plants (largely because they are so often grown as houseplants under conditions that could never lead to blooming), cacti are capable of producing some of the most exciting flowers of any plants. The period of bloom may be brief, however— as brief as a single night for the night-blooming cereus.

Cacti rank among the best greenhouse plants, as many growers well know. They like the full intensity of light and heat that the environment can offer, and are well able to tolerate the coolness and high humidity that can also occur. Some of the best of them are small and floriferous, and they make few demands on the gardener in return for the pleasure they bring.

Astrophytum myriostigma

Mamillaria 'Pink Nymph'

Echinocereus engelmannii

Rebutia minuscula

Echinocereus engelmannii

Native to southwestern United States and Mexico. Grows to 16 inches. Thick stems with upright, branched form and long spines. Yellow, pink, or red flowers.

E. pectinatus (rainbow cactus)   Grows to 12 inches. The yellow and pink stripes that band the thick stems account for the popular name. Fragrant pink flowers.

Echinopsis, Lobivia, Parodia, Rebutia

Grow to 6 inches; bloom at 2 inches. A quartet of South American genera of very similar overall appearance, any species of which is well suited for greenhouse growing. They are low-growing, globular or cylindrical, easygoing, and free-flowering—the definitive potted cactus. They are readily raised from seed, blooming in

about 4 years, and can be increased by detaching the offsets that form around the base.

Echinopsis multiplex: fragrant pink flowers.

Lobivia hertrichiana: bright red flowers.

Parodia chrysacanthion: yellow flowers; hardy to 12° F.

Rebutia minuscula: crimson flowers; hardy to 12° F.

Mammillaria hahniana
Old-lady cactus

Native to Mexico. Grows to 4 inches. As much admired for its dense, intricate white spines as for the relatively small violet-red flowers.

Neoporteria chilensis

Grows to 10 inches. Becomes columnar with age, and is distinct among these group 2 cacti in bearing its red, pink, or yellow flowers in fall.

Opuntia

Although among the most familiar of cacti, this genus is in many species quite awkward for the greenhouse, being large or wickedly spined or both. *O. microdasys* (bunny-ears), the *Opuntia* most frequently encountered, reaches 3 feet and is armed not with obvious spines but with more treacherous tiny barbs or glochids, skin-piercing and intensely irritating. It is very distinctive, however, and mature plants bear large, pale yellow flowers.

Caladium

Family *Araceae*. Native to South America. Deciduous. Colorful foliage plants, chiefly grown in the form of one species:

C. × *hortulanum* (usually with *C. bicolor* as one parent; angel's-wings)   Grows to between 6 and 18 inches. Warmth-loving plant with leaves banded in shades of

red, pink, bronze, silver, and green. Primarily grown in summer, in pots or bedded in the ground, because of its need for temperatures above 70° F. The season can be made earlier or later in a greenhouse that is warm enough. For summer show start into growth in March, using a loose, fibrous medium of sand, leaf mold, and peat moss with a generous portion of fertilizer. Feed and water regularly during the growing season. Withhold water when the leaves begin to die back. Store dry over winter at 50° to 60° F. Susceptible to slugs and snails. Propagate by dividing the tubers as new growth begins.

Calceolaria crenatiflora

See *Annuals*

Calendula officinalis

See *Annuals*

Calliandra haematocephala

Camellia sasanqua 'Chansonette'

Camellia 'Higo Nioi Fubuki'

Camellia sasanqua

Calliandra

Family *Leguminosae*. Native to tropical America. Evergreen shrubs. Primarily grown in greenhouses is one species:

C. haematocephala;
C. inaequilatera (pink-powderpuff) Grows to 10 feet. A delightful container plant with a willowy, erect form given naturally to espaliering. Fine-cut, almost feathery foliage; large puffs of pink flowers bloom through the winter. Readily kept to pot size by pruning. Enjoys the brightness and warmth of the greenhouse if given plenty of water during the summer; otherwise standard culture. Susceptible to mealybugs. Best at a minimum temperature of 45° F, but does well enough down to freezing and even 2 to 3 degrees below. Propagate by cuttings.

Camellia
Camellia

Family *Theaceae*. Native to Asia, in particular China and Japan. Evergreen trees and shrubs ranging in size from 2 to 30 feet, depending on species and variety. However, all begin flowering when quite small, 3 feet or less, and so are suitable for pot culture.

The camellias are among the best greenhouse plants—attractive in form and foliage at all times, spectacular when in bloom in fall or winter, and in most cases particularly well suited to greenhouse growing, preferring hot conditions in summer and cold in winter. Standard cultural conditions. Somewhat susceptible to mealybugs and, to a lesser degree, to scale. Readily propagated by cuttings taken in summer and by seeds, although varieties do not come true from seed. Seeds should be put in a closed container with a damp medium such as sphagnum moss and kept in a warm place; examine frequently for germination.

There are at least 31 species of *Camellia*, of which 5 (along with numerous hybrids) are commonly grown as ornamentals: *C. chrysantha*, *C. japonica*, *C. lutchuensis*, *C. reticulata*, and *C. sasanqua*. *C. japonica*, however, remains far and away the best known, and is synonymous with camellia to many.

C. chrysantha Unique in the genus for its yellow flowers. It is a relatively recent introduction that is more likely to be valuable as a parent of hybrids than as an ornamental in its own right. It has relatively small flowers, an awkward, rangy habit of growth, and uncertain cultural requirements. Best in cool conditions, down to 32° F, but has little hardiness below that.

C. japonica This is the touchstone to which the other species are compared. It is made up of innumerable varieties that differ primarily in

flower color (pink, red, or white), flower size and form, and flowering time, but also to some extent in plant size, shape, and growth rate. Depending on the variety, flowering time ranges from December to March, although all varieties bloom later under cooler conditions. A typical *C. japonica* grows to 25 feet in nature. In the greenhouse pruning can keep it within bounds for an indefinite but not infinite time. Pot culture slows the rate of growth compared to growing in the ground. Cultivars that naturally grow slowly include 'Cardinal's Cap' (cardinal red flowers), 'Black Domino' (very dark red flowers), and 'Nuccio's Jewel' (white flowers shaded to pink).

C. japonica appears to be the hardiest of the five common species. (Another species, *C. oleifera*, is probably hardier but is a far less attractive plant.) It survives and flowers down to 4° F under glass, although flowering time is delayed until May. Although the

Cantua buxifolia

Ceropegia woodii

closed buds are as impervious to cold as the leaves, the flowers are damaged by a few degrees of frost and are protected by a mechanism that keeps the buds closed until prolonged warmth suggests it is safe to open.

There are two groupings of *C. japonica* distinctive enough to have received their own names. Higo camellias bloom profusely and drop their flowers all in one piece. *C. rusticana*, the snow camellia, comes from the cool mountains of Japan where it is protected by a blanket of snow in winter. It has proved less tolerant of winter cold and summer heat than other cultivars.

C. lutchuensis   Grows to 4 feet. Bears small, white, fragrant flowers in winter. Good for pot culture because of its size but relatively temperamental and tender; survives down to a few degrees below freezing. It has given rise to a hybrid, 'Fragrant Pink', that is just as small and fragrant and a good deal easier to grow.

C. reticulata   Grows to 30 to 35 feet. Like a larger, rangier *C. japonica*, and thus that much more difficult to contain in a greenhouse. However, among its varieties are some of the most spectacular flowers of the genus, with the same color range and time of flowering as *C. japonica* but tending to be larger. Less hardy than *C. japonica*; however, a hybrid, 'Lila Naff', succeeds at 12° F.

C. sasanqua   Smaller and denser than *C. japonica*, with smaller, less profuse flowers in shades of red, white, and pink. Fall blooming; hardy to 12° F or somewhat lower. Will hold buds closed until spring if cold intervenes. Well suited to the greenhouse because of its size, which ranges from 6 feet for 'Yuletide' down to 2 feet for 'Shishi-gashira'.

Cantua

Family *Polemoniaceae*. Native to South America. Evergreen shrubs, one of which is in greenhouse cultivation:

C. buxifolia (Sacred-flower-of-the-Incas)   Grows to 10 feet. A slender, vinelike plant that can be treated as a vine, tucked tidily against a wall of the greenhouse. Clusters of brilliant red tubular flowers are borne in late winter and early spring and sporadically throughout the year, presenting a magnificent display at their peak. Leaves are small and nondescript; growth is open and somewhat unkempt, inviting pruning, which should be done after the main period of flowering. Standard culture, though shading should be provided in summer if kept in the greenhouse. Minimum temperature 45° F. Propagate by cuttings.

Cattleya

See *Orchids*

Centradenia

Family *Melastomataceae*. Native to Mexico and Central America. Evergreen, soft-stemmed subshrubs, one of which is grown in greenhouses and as a houseplant:

C. floribunda   Grows to 2 feet. A bushy container plant with linear, pointed leaves tinged with red on the underside and clusters of rose pink flowers. Cultural requirements are similar to those for begonias, with standard soil, watering, and feeding; requires a minimum temperature of 50° F, and protection from the fiercest summer sun. Propagate by cuttings.

Ceropegia

Family *Asclepiadaceae*. Native to tropics from Africa to Australia. Evergreen and deciduous perennials, sometimes vining, often succulent. Flowers intriguing in their

Chorizema cordatum

× *Citrofortunella mitis*

odd and busy shape and mixtures of subdued colors. Very good in pots, including hanging pots. Standard culture, with particular care not to overwater in winter. Susceptible to mealybugs. Propagate by seed or by stem cuttings. Minimum temperature 45° F.

C. dichotoma Native to the Canary Islands. Grows to 3 feet. Deciduous. A clump of upright, white, rushlike stems topped by a fringe of leaves. Much different from *C. sandersonii* and *C. woodii*, and less readily available, but a striking container plant even when out of leaf, which is a good part of the time. Bears relatively large (¾ inch) yellow flowers in the nodes of the stems. *C. fusca* is similar in effect, but is shorter (18 inches), and its flowers are yellow marked with brown.

C. sandersonii (parachuteplant) Native to South Africa. Grows to 6 feet. Trailing plant with succulent leaves and stems. Can be trained as a climber to best show off the remarkable greenish flowers, which flare at the top to suggest a parachute.

C. woodii (string-of-hearts; rosaryvine) Native to South Africa. Grows to 2 feet. The most commonly grown. Very slender stems with equally spaced pairs of thick, heart-shaped leaves lightly marbled with white. The flowers are small and a dull purple but worth a second, closer look. Grown to best advantage in a hanging pot.

Chorizema

Family *Leguminosae*. Native to Australia. Small, prickly-leaved evergreen shrubs of lax, open growth that permits training as a vine. Very good for pot culture, although the wide reaching leaves easily become snared in clothing. Drought tolerant but not harmed by a standard watering routine if well drained; one of the few plants entirely comfortable in the greenhouse in the heat of summer. Unaffected by pests and diseases. Full sun to light shade. Requires little feeding. Summer cuttings root readily but are slow to establish and need extra shading and watering.

C. cordatum The most readily available, this has clashing red and orange pea flowers in abundance from mid-March until May. Performs well down to 32° F but is sensitive to frost. Five feet high and as wide at maturity but readily pruned; blooms at 8 to 10 inches.

Chrysanthemum

See *Annuals*

Cineraria (Senecio cruentus)

See *Annuals*

Citrus and Fortunella

Family *Rutaceae*. Native to Asia. Evergreen woody plants. Many of the aspects of choosing greenhouse plants come together in this group. On the plus side they are familiar, attractive, amenable, and available; they bear fruit, and they have fragrant blooms in winter. On the negative side they are, to some, too familiar and the fruit commonplace; they are basically good-sized trees, and they are quite susceptible to insect attack. And yet the outcome of the equation is never in doubt: They are among the most appreciated plants for the greenhouse, well worth the extra effort they might demand.

Citrus and *Fortunella* require full sun to light shade, standard soil, copious watering in the growing season, and feeding in equal

Clerodendrum fragrans

Clerodendrum nutans

increments in late winter, June, and August. They are readily pruned, which is one of the reasons they serve so well as container plants; another reason is that they flower and fruit when astonishingly small. They are attacked by aphids, scale, and mealybugs; they can develop iron chlorosis. Chlorosis—yellowed leaves with green veins—can be remedied with chelated iron or iron sulfate. They thrive in heat over the summer but are nonetheless best moved outside because of their susceptibility to pests. They can tolerate a surprising amount of winter cold, though there is a great range in this from species to species. From least to most tolerant are: lime (minimum temperature 28° F), grapefruit, lemon, tangelo, sweet orange, mandarin orange (tangerine), Meyer lemon, sour orange, *Fortunella* (kumquat), calamondin, and 'Chang-sha'

tangerine (minimum temperature 15° F). The fruit of all, however, is likely to be damaged at 28° F. Propagation is by cuttings (except *Fortunella*), grafting, and seed. Seedlings will not come true for most named varieties, and in fact are likely to turn out to be thorny monsters that never bloom.

× *Citrofortunella mitis* (Calamondin)   The citrus most often grown on windowsills. Naturally small and shapely, easily kept to less than 2 feet. Flowers and bears heavily; the fruit is sour but can be used for marmalade.

Citrus medica × limon (Ponderosa lemon)   Large lemons on a tiny plant, though it will in time reach 3 feet high and 4 feet across. Very good for pot culture.

Citrus meyeri (Meyer lemon)   Smaller fruits on a more cold-hardy plant, otherwise similar to and as rewarding as the Ponderosa. The fruit is much less acid than most lemons and the skin color is more orange.

Citrus reticulata (mandarin orange, or tangerine) Grows into a 10- to 15-foot tree. 'Dancy', a standard variety, begins bearing at 18 inches. 'Chang-sha', perhaps the hardiest *Citrus*, is usually raised from seed (coming true) and does not bloom until 5 to 6 feet.

Citrus sinensis (sweet orange)   Grows to 15 feet. 'Valencia', a standard juice orange, begins bearing when less than 24 inches.

Fortunella (kumquat) Because it is naturally smaller, this is a better container plant than *Citrus*, but the fruit is less generally appreciated, being traditionally reserved for the Christmas season. However, eaten whole, skin and fruit combine to make a distinctive flavor combination of sweet and sour. *Fortunella margarita* 'Nagami' is the standard kumquat; *F. hindsii* is even smaller, with tiny fruits, but the fruit is not edible.

Clerodendrum

Family *Verbenaceae*. Native to tropical Asia. Evergreen vines and shrubs of easy culture that bear showy red or white flowers. Leaves are rounded and attractive; growth is rapid and dense. Good in pots; vigorous in the ground. Need pruning in early spring. Standard culture. Susceptible to mealybugs and spider mites. Propagate by cuttings or layers in summer. Best at a minimum temperature above 40° F.

C. fragrans   Shrub. Grows to 6 feet. Bears strongly scented white flowers in terminal corymbs in late summer and fall.

C. nutans   Shrub. Grows to 6 feet. Bears pendulous white flowers in fall.

C. speciosissimum (Javaglorybower)   Shrub. Grows to 6 feet. Minimum temperature 50° F. Bears scarlet flowers in summer. Widely grown.

Clerodendrum thomsoniae

Coleus thyrsoideus

C. splendens   Vine. Grows to 10 feet. Bears scarlet flowers in fall and winter. Twiner; needs support.

C. thomsoniae (glorybower)   Vine. Grows to 15 feet. Bears red flowers set off by inflated white calyx in late summer and fall. A vigorous and attractive plant; a good way to bring quick impact to a greenhouse. Twiner.

Codiaeum

Croton

Family *Euphorbiaceae*. Native to Polynesia. Evergreen shrubs. The emphasis on flowering plants in the greenhouse need not be overdone when there are such vivid, colorful foliage plants as the crotons. Full sun to partial shade; standard soil, moist in the growing season; and a warm, moist atmosphere. Much less watering and humidity in the winter; minimum temperature 60° F. Frequent feeding while growing for potbound plants. Propagate by cuttings, or by seeds to create new varieties.

C. variegatum   The only species generally grown. Grows to 3 feet, more or less, depending on variety. Long, leathery, richly colored leaves and a many-stemmed habit of growth. Insignificant axillary flowers may be produced. There are many varieties, in shades of orange, pink, red, and yellow. Naming is quite confused, and plants are perhaps best bought on the basis of catalog descriptions or, in a nursery, by sight.

Codonanthe aurora

See *Gesneriads*

Coleonema and Diosma

Family *Rutaceae*. Native to South Africa. Evergreen shrubs that are closely related, very similar, and often confused in the trade. They have fragrant, heathlike foliage; a slender, upright, arching form; and white or pink flowers in late winter. They reach 5 feet or more but are amenable to pot culture, being naturally restrained and readily pruned. For compact form, shear after blooming. Standard culture, except somewhat susceptible to overwatering. Hardy to 25° F, perhaps lower. Propagated by seeds or by cuttings taken in summer.

Coleonema pulchrum   Pink flowers.

Diosma ericoides   White flowers. Nursery plants are in fact often the similar *D. alba*.

Coleus

Family *Labiatae*. Native to tropical Africa and Asia. Softstemmed subshrubs. Evergreen, if green is the right word for the brilliantly colored foliage of some species. Easily grown container plants. Standard culture but definitely move outdoors into some shade over the summer. Susceptible to aphids, mealybugs, and whiteflies. Propagate by cuttings, which can be done in water. Minimum temperature 45° F.

C. blumei var. *verschaffeltii* (florist's coleus) Native to Java. Grows to 2 feet. Richly patterned and colored leaves make this an excellent pot and bedding plant. Typically grown as an outdoor garden plant, often started from seed each spring, but the plants can continue to give satisfaction if brought into the greenhouse before the first frost. May grow leggy, which, with the help of tip pruning, corrects itself when new growth commences in the spring. As good a strategy is to take cuttings, which will be serviceable ornamentals even while rooting. Spikes of blue flowers may appear toward the end of summer; they sometimes detract more from the shape of the plant than they add as flowers.

C. thyrsoideus   Native to central Africa. Grows to 3 feet. Grown for its flowers, which are blue and borne in panicles in fall and winter.

Correa decumbens

Crossandra infundibuliformis

Convolvulus cneorum

Columnea

See *Gesneriads*

Convolvulus

Family *Convolvulaceae*. A widespread family that includes the dwarf morning glory (*C. tricolor*). One species is of interest for the greenhouse:

C. cneorum Grows to 4 feet. Evergreen. One of the most silver of shrubs and an instant focus of attention as a container plant. White morning glory flowers, borne in summer, somehow stand out from and complement the foliage. Vigorous grower but easily restrained by pruning, which will supply material for indoor arrangements. Standard culture, but avoid wetting the leaves when watering in winter. Propagate by cuttings. Hardy to 18° F.

Correa

Australian fuchsia

Family *Rutaceae*. In actuality, not at all related to *Fuchsia*. Native to Australia. Evergreen shrubs, one of which is often grown in greenhouses:

C. reflexa (*C. pulchella*, *C. speciosa*; also listed as *C. decumbens*) Grows to 3 to 6 feet. An excellent container plant, readily pruned and of restrained growth. Flowers when small and bears its flowers from November to April. Its red flowers resemble long pendant bells, and are bright and cheery. An effective tall cover planted in the ground, dense and spreading. Standard culture. Propagate by cuttings. Hardy to 20° F.

Crassula

See *Succulents*

Crocus

See *Bulbs for Forcing*

Crossandra

Family *Acanthaceae*. Native to tropics from Africa to India. Evergreen shrubs, one of which is a common greenhouse plant:

C. infundibuliformis (firecracker-plant) Native to India. Grows to 3 feet. An easy, dependable, attractive container plant. Glossy, dark green leaves form a backdrop for dense spikes of orange-red flowers through much of the summer. Blooms when small, less than 1 foot; can reach flowering size in 6 months from seed. Standard culture, with a warm location. Minimum temperature 50° F. Susceptible to mealybugs. Propagate by cuttings as well as by seed.

Cuphea

Family *Lythraceae*. Native to tropical America. Evergreen subshrubs. Grow to 1 to 2 feet. Trim, easily grown container plants. Standard culture, with plenty of water and some shade in summer. Best at a

minimum temperature of 50° F, but will go to 40° F or somewhat lower without harm. Pinch the growing tips of younger plants; prune older ones severely after flowering. Propagate by seed and cuttings.

C. hyssopifolia (false-heather) Compact bushy form, tending to be broader than tall. Small, pink, purple, or white flowers, borne in summer, are profuse enough to give the effect of a haze of color against a background of long, narrow leaves.

C. ignea (cigarplant) Similar in form and foliage to *C. hyssopifolia*. The flowers are much brighter, a glowing red; dark and white rings at the end combine with the shape to suggest the common name. Again, the flowers are tiny, but they stand out sharply against the foliage to give a colorful effect.

Cuphea hyssopifolia

Cyclamen persicum

Cyclamen

Family *Primulaceae*. Native to the lands around the Mediterranean. Tuberous-rooted, summer-dormant perennials. They are among the choicest of greenhouse container plants, for the distinctive reflexed flowers borne in autumn, winter, or spring and the shapely leaves that are often etched with silver. The flowers come in shades of red, pink, or white, and are sometimes wonderfully fragrant. The flowers are small for all species except *C. persicum*, the florist's cyclamen.

Culture is easier for some species than for others, but all are to some degree demanding, specifically in terms of their summer resting period, when they need to be dry or at least well drained. When in leaf they require good light, well-drained soil, and regular feeding and watering. They are propagated by seed, which tends to germinate at the time

of year when the leaves normally appear. Plants take 2 to 4 years to reach blooming size. There are reports of propagation by dividing the tubers, particularly for *C. persicum*, but they are not well substantiated. Hardiness varies according to species, from frost-tender to hardy outdoors in zone 6 (see map, page 36). The hardier ones do best in a subfreezing greenhouse but nonetheless are thoroughly satisfactory in a warmer one. Somewhat susceptible to mealybugs and scale.

C. cilicium Grows to 4 to 6 inches. Hardy to 12° F. Fall-blooming. Fragrant pale pink flowers blotched with purple. Not difficult to oversummer but should be protected from excessive watering.

C. coum Grows to 4 to 6 inches. Hardy to 0° F. A vast tribe of varieties, subspecies, and related species, with a correspondingly large spread of flowering times, from December to March (also blooming later in a colder environment). Easy to grow,

succeeding in an open garden environment. Flowers red or pink; leaves rounded and, in some varieties, heavily patterned.

C. graecum Grows to 8 inches. Hardy to 12° F. Robust; develops a large tuber. Prefers a drier spot than most of the others and requires a strong drying over the summer. Patterned leaves; pale to deep pink flowers in October and November.

C. hederifolium (*C. neapolitanum*) Grows to 6 inches. Hardy to 0° F or below; one of the easiest to grow. Rose pink flowers and, as the name implies, ivy-shaped leaves. Likely to self-sow.

C. libanoticum Grows to 6 inches. Hardy to 32° F. Pale pink, delicately blotched, very fragrant flowers. Not easy to grow; some dryness required in summer, and protection from intense heating.

C. persicum (florist's cyclamen; Persian-violet) Grows to 8 to 10 inches. Hardy to 32° F. The most common of the genus and yet the most difficult to grow, or at least to keep going. It comes on readily from seed, blooming in 2 to 3 years, but is then touchy. Some growers put the pots on their sides in a shady spot over the summer, resuming watering when new leaves begin to show. Probably more commonly the plants are discarded after the single season of bloom. Still, they are wonderful plants, blooming majestically, unfurling into the downturned flowers typical of the genus. The number of varieties is legend, distinguished by size, color of flower (red, pink, white, or mixtures), fragrance, and leaf markings.

C. purpurascens (*C. europaeum*) Grows to 4 to 6 inches. Hardy to 0° F. Fragrant crimson flowers in July and August. Very brief dormancy. A woodland plant that is stunning where it succeeds but has

Daphne odora

Dichorisandra thyrsiflora

proved to be somewhat difficult—the tubers may be particularly attractive to various burrowers.

   C. repandum   Grows to 4 to 6 inches. Hardy to 12° F. Crimson flowers in spring; the latest blooming species. Ivy-shaped, marbled leaves.

Cymbidium

See *Orchids*

Daphne

Family *Thymelaeaceae*. Native to the temperate zones of Europe and Asia. Evergreen and deciduous shrubs. A genus noted for the delicious fragrance of its flowers, and also for the sudden, inexplicable demise of individual plants. Basic culture nonetheless is straightforward: good light but protection from the hottest sun; good drainage; regular feeding and watering when in growth. There are many fine species but only one is normally grown in greenhouses:

   D. odora (winter daphne)   Native to China and Japan. Grows to 4 feet or larger. Evergreen. Variety 'Alba Marginata' is hardy to 12° F (and is distinctively attractive, with variegated leaves). The February daphne is an outstanding plant for the greenhouse, in a pot or in the ground, filling the air in January and February with the fragrance of its small pink flowers. It can become uncomfortably large but begins blooming when small, is readily pruned, and is easily propagated by cuttings. It has a treelike form, and the thick, leathery leaves are attractive. It will withstand some degree of drought, and indeed is considered to bloom better after a dry summer. It has little of the propensity to sudden death of some of the other species, although overwatering in the summer may lead to root molds, and it is fairly susceptible to mealybugs. It thrives under cool winter conditions, doing well in a subfreezing greenhouse and tending to bloom more dependably there than in a warmer one.

Davallia fejeensis

See *Ferns*

Dendrobium

See *Orchids*

Dianthus caryophyllus

See *Annuals*

Dichorisandra

Family *Commelinaceae*. Native to tropical America. Evergreen, cane-stemmed plants; one species is valuable for house and greenhouse:

   D. thyrsiflora (blue-ginger)   Grows to 4 feet. A rugged, robust plant with dense racemes of blue to blue-purple flowers in late fall and early winter. Additionally valuable for its lanceolate, richly colored leaves and the distinctive shape formed by

its erect, close, sparsely leaved stems. A fast grower in the ground but well behaved as a container plant. Of very easy culture, indifferent to soil and drought tolerant. Feed regularly in summer for good growth and flowering. Best with some protection from the sun; will in fact succeed in quite deep shade. Minimum temperature 60° F. Susceptible to mealybugs. Propagate by division in spring or stem cuttings in summer.

Diosma

See *Coleonema*

Dombeya

Family *Byttneriaceae*. Native to Africa and neighboring islands. Evergreen shrubs. Good for providing a tropical look to a larger greenhouse. Wide, palmate leaves and ball-shaped flower clusters dangle from the branches. Fast growing but easily pruned. Prune after flowering; at the same time remove spent flower clusters,

Dombeya × *cayeuxii*

Erodium chamaedryoides 'Roseum'

which tend to be untidy. Standard culture; minimum temperature 50° F. Susceptible to mealybugs. Propagate by cuttings.

D. × *cayeuxii (D. burgessiae* × *wallichii)* (pinkball dombeya)   Grows to 15 feet in the ground; readily kept to 6 feet in a container. Leaves almost a foot across; pink flowers borne in winter.

Drosanthemum

See *Succulents*

Echeveria

See *Succulents*

Echinocereus engelmannii

See *Cactaceae*

Echinocereus pectinatus

See *Cactaceae*

Echinopsis

See *Cactaceae*

Epidendrum

See *Orchids*

Epiphyllum ackermannii hybrids

See *Cactaceae*

Eriobotrya

Family *Rosaceae*. Native to warm temperate Asia. Evergreen. One species is commonly grown in the greenhouse:

E. japonica (loquat) Grows to 25 feet. A splendid plant for any greenhouse that can fit it in. Has large, distinguished, oval leaves and sweet, acidic yellow fruit in clusters that can add up to a substantial harvest on a mature plant. The fruits can be used to prepare preserves or chutney. It bears dull white, fragrant but not showy flowers in fall. Treelike form. Standard culture; drought resistant when established. An excellent ornamental container plant when small; becomes leggy, however, as it reaches fruit-bearing size. Can be pruned readily and container culture will slow its growth, but it may outgrow its space in time. Thinning branches aids fruit production. Grafting on quince stock results in a dwarfed plant. Somewhat susceptible to mealybugs. Propagate by summer cuttings or by seeds; seeds result in plants of uncertain fruit quality. Named, grafted varieties include 'Champagne', which bears tart fruit and is best in a warm-summer area, and 'Gold Nugget', which bears sweeter fruit and can mature fruit under cooler conditions. Hardy to at least 12° F, but temperatures below 20° F may damage fruit, and flowers will not set fruit below 28° F.

Erodium

Family *Geraniaceae*. Widespread. Evergreen and deciduous herbaceous plants. Part of a trio of closely related genera that also includes *Geranium* and *Pelargonium*. There are a number of species, but only one is commonly grown in the greenhouse:

E. chamaedryoides (E. reichardii)   Grows to 3 inches. Evergreen herbaceous perennial from the Balearic Islands. A dense, slowly spreading mound of small, neat leaves topped for an incredibly long period, from mid-spring into autumn, by a gentle haze of pink or white flowers; it is out of flower for only the three winter months. A good container plant, particularly in company with other similarly restrained species. Full sun or light shade, but protect from excessive heat. Needs good drainage; undemanding of feeding and watering. Hardy to 12° F; does best under the coolest conditions. Propagate by cuttings or divisions treated as cuttings.

Eucalyptus macrocarpa

Eucalyptus torquata

Eucalyptus
Gum tree

Family *Myrtaceae*. Native to Australia and adjacent regions. Evergreen trees and shrubs. Called gum because of the resin, known as kino, that is commercially extracted from some species; other common names include box, messmate, yate, mallee, and sally. Much beloved for their foliage, which in general is long and willowlike, though in many species the juvenile foliage is round. Leaves are of a solid texture, often blue-green, and to one degree or another redolent of the odor of eucalyptus. They are also thought to have medicinal value, and can certainly add pungency to tea or stew.

Although the majority of the more than five hundred species are sizable trees, the genus offers a number of excellent plants for the greenhouse. Many of the best flowerers are also relatively small but are not hardy, whereas the species that will endure considerable cold (and at least one will go down to 0° F under glass) belong to the tree-sized, white-flowered group. Several of these, however, have good form when young and serve as striking container plants for four or five years, after which they can be bedded out for their final summer.

Not affected by pests except for possible minor aphid infestations on new growth. Difficult to transplant. Able to take summer heat in the greenhouse if well watered; otherwise standard watering and minimal feeding. Full sun to part shade. Propagation is by seeds only. A large proportion of the seeds are naturally sterile; a seed packet will therefore contain a large number of seeds.

E. eximia (golden gum) Tree-sized; 6 to 7 feet after growing six years in a pot. Distinct in having mature-type foliage when young. Leaves are striking: heavy, spear-shaped, and gray-green but only slightly fragrant. Attractive heads of yellow flowers may be borne by larger (greater than 10 feet) plants. Hardy to 20° F.

E. glaucescens (Tingiringi gum) Tree-sized; 8 feet after growing four years in a pot. Very good form; gray foliage; very fragrant; very drought resistant; also very fast growing. A particularly good species for bedding out. Hardy to 12° F. *E. rubida* is similar, but has green leaves rather than gray. May bear rather small white flowers when large.

E. gunnii (cider gum) Tree-sized; 10 feet after growing seven years in the ground in a cold environment. Appears to be the hardiest species, to 0° F. Fragrant, round, almost white leaves. Flowers are small and creamy white, borne only on larger plants.

E. macrocarpa (bluebush) Small; flowers at 4 feet. Grows to 5 feet in four years in the ground. Perhaps the best species for flowering; huge rose-red flowers sporting prominent yellow stamens are borne primarily in the summer. Leaves are large, round, and slightly fragrant. Form is sprawling and contorted and somewhat difficult to deal with, although tying the ends of the branches to overhead supports can be effective. Drought sensitive but not heat sensitive. Hardy to 28° F.

E. moorei nana   Small; 2½ feet after growing four years in a pot. Ultimate height 9 feet. It is best considered a foliage plant; the flowers, if they appear, are small and creamy white. Green, linear leaves are somewhat fragrant. Heat and drought sensitive. Hardy to 12° F.

E. torquata (coral gum) Grows to 20 feet in nature but tends to stabilize at 6 to 7 feet in the greenhouse; reaches 4 feet after growing five years in a pot. Another good flowering species. The individual flowers are much smaller than those of *E. macrocarpa* but are borne in clusters. They are pink and appear in late winter and spring. The foliage is linear and somewhat fragrant; the form is upright and narrow. Hardy to 28° F.

Syzygium jambos

Euphorbia fulgens

Evolvulus glomeratus

Eucharis

Family *Amaryllidaceae*. Native to South America. Stately bulbous plants.

E. grandiflora (Amazon-lily)   Grows to 2 feet. Evergreen. A dependable and distinguished container plant with solid, arching, strap-shaped leaves that always look good, and fragrant, tubular white flowers in summer. Off-season bloom can be induced by reducing water sharply after the current set of leaves has grown and matured. Otherwise standard culture. Minimum temperature 55° to 60° F. Propagate by seeds or by removing offsets in spring and potting them up.

Eugenia

Family *Myrtaceae*. Native to all tropics. A large genus of evergreen trees and shrubs of greatest interest for their lustrous green, solid foliage and, in some cases, their edible fruit. White flowers are not particularly showy.

E. uniflora (pitanga, Surinam-cherry)   Native to Brazil. Grows to 25 feet in nature but can readily be kept to 6 feet in the greenhouse. The small, red to yellow fruit are sweet and juicy, and not commercially available. Foliage and treelike form are also very attractive; flowers are small but fragrant. Grows slowly in a pot and is amenable to pruning. Standard culture. Propagate by seed or cuttings. Tolerates temperatures down to 32° F but better above 40° F. Very similar is the closely related *Syzygium jambos* (roseapple or Malabar-plum). It also bears edible fruit.

Euphorbia

Family *Euphorbiaceae*. Worldwide. A large family of evergreen and deciduous, herbaceous and shrublike plants. Of the many that are well suited to the greenhouse, most are succulents (see Succulents, page 99). The following two species, which are not succulents, require warmth (minimum temperature 55° to 60° F) and are quite drought tolerant though they flourish with summer watering. Otherwise they require standard culture, with restricted watering in winter. Somewhat susceptible to mealybugs. Propagated by cuttings in summer. Take care to avoid the sap, which may be irritating to the skin or poisonous if ingested.

E. fulgens (scarlet-plume)   Native to Mexico. Grows to 4 feet. Evergreen. A striking plant at all times—slender, graceful, and arching, with solid, bright green leaves distributed rather sparsely along the stems. The effect is intensified in winter, when long sprays of orange or scarlet bracts appear, adding a bright, colorful note. Can be somewhat difficult in cultivation, resenting over- or underwatering, disturbance of the roots, and drafts, but is worth the effort. Easily placed despite its height because of its narrow form.

E. milii (*E. splendens*) (crown-of-thorns)   Native to Malagasy. Grows to 2 to 3 feet. Evergreen. Thorny enough to demand respect in handling, but compact enough when small to be a good container plant. Blooms when no more than 10 inches high. Climbing stems require support, such as a trellis, when larger. Bracts are yellow, orange, pink, or red, depending on variety, and are borne nearly all year. Leaves are sparse and carried primarily on the ends of branches.

Evolvulus

Family *Convolvulaceae*. Native to the tropical Americas. Evergreen subshrubs, one of which is commonly grown in the greenhouse:

E. glomeratus   Grows to 18 inches. A splendid plant for the warmer greenhouse. (It will survive at 32° F but not flourish.) It carries its relatively large, soft blue flowers for much of the year. Slow, restrained growth and small ultimate size suit it well for

Feijoa sellowiana

Felicia amelloides

container growing and for combining with other such species in containers. Upright, sparsely branched. Standard culture; very tolerant. Propagate by cuttings in spring or summer.

Exacum

Family *Gentianaceae*. Native to tropical Asia. Evergreen herbaceous plants, one of which is a greenhouse favorite:

E. affine (German-violet)   Grows to 10 inches. An annual or short-lived perennial that gives great value as a container plant during its span, covering itself with flowers during the summer months. The star-shaped flowers are blue with prominent yellow stamens and are fragrant. Standard culture, but feed and water well to hasten growth. Seed usually sown in spring for a summer display, but a greenhouse permits a fall sowing for both earlier and longer bloom.

Feijoa

Family *Myrtaceae*. A single species, the pineapple guava, is grown in the greenhouse. (For other guavas, see *Psidium,* page 94.)

F. sellowiana (pineapple guava)   Native to South America. Grows to 18 feet. Evergreen. Although its ultimate size is too large for most greenhouses, it is so amenable to pruning and training that it is quite realistic to grow it in a pot, where it can readily be kept to 6 feet. Valuable for its distinctive fruit and also for its flowers, red with vivid red stamens, that are borne in May and June. The fleshy petals themselves are edible. Long, glossy green leaves. Drought tolerant but does well under standard culture. Minimum temperature 32° F or lower; branches may be killed by frost but will resprout. Pruning should be done in spring. Best propagated by cuttings or grafting; seedlings may produce inferior fruit. Self-fertile varieties are 'Coolidge' and 'Pineapple Gem'.

Felicia

Family *Compositae*. Native to tropical and southern Africa. Annuals and evergreen subshrubs. The following subshrub is excellent in the greenhouse, where it has the impact of a herbaceous perennial:

F. amelloides (blue-marguerite)   Grows to 1½ feet, with 4-foot spread. Evergreen. Yellow-centered blue flower heads are borne in abundance for a long period, in fact continuously under warmer conditions. The leaves are broad and rounded and slightly fragrant. It is primarily the foliage that distinguishes this species from *Brachycome multiflora* (see page 52), whose flowers have a very similar impact, although those of the *Felicia* are a brighter blue. Excellent in pots, including hanging pots; invaluable for bedding in the ground. Vigorous, and ragged-looking if not pruned; prune in late summer to encourage a flush of winter bloom. Standard culture with extra attention to watering in summer. Propagate by seeds and cuttings. Varieties include 'George Lewis', with dark blue flowers; 'San Luis', with unusually large flowers; and 'Astrid Thomas', compact and with flowers less dependent on sun to open. Readily withstands 32° F, but a minimum temperature of 45° to 50° is necessary for winter bloom.

Ferns

Evergreen and deciduous, herbaceous and treelike, cosmopolitan in distribution, ferns are nonetheless unified in their impact as elegant foliage plants. Their cultural requirements are also diverse, but the majority of species of interest for the greenhouse do in fact want what ferns are

Ferns

Garden planning usually focuses on flowers and their glorious colors, but, like it or not, garden appreciation is often by necessity an appreciation of various shades of green. Foliage is present for months or forever; flowers are fleeting. It is wise, therefore, to concentrate on foliage as much as bloom.

The appeal of ferns, since they do not flower, lies entirely in their foliage, in the clean geometry (and sometimes the striking shades) of their fronds. Their appeal, it must be admitted, is somewhat static; there are no dramatic changes. Therefore, in many situations ferns serve best as a background, providing an ever-pleasing setting for flowering plants. And yet changes do occur. Tight new fiddleheads peep from the crown of mature foliage and slowly, majestically, unroll and expand into shining fresh fronds.

Ferns seize the imagination as well as the eye. Food of dinosaurs, generator of coal, primitive yet enduring, they can contribute mightily to creating within the greenhouse a world out of time.

Blechnum gibbum

Adiantum tenerum

Davallia fejeensis

Platycerium bifurcatum

expected to want: shade, humidity, and warmth. They serve well as background plants for the protected crannies out of direct sun, though all of them are well worth a closer look. Some also do well as houseplants, but in general they need the high humidity of the greenhouse to do their best. Standard soil and feeding; copious watering. Mealybugs may get at the undersides of the fronds, and snails and slugs can cause damage. Propagate by spores or division.

Adiantum tenerum

Family *Polypodiaceae*. Native to American tropics. Grows to 2 feet. Evergreen. One of many excellent maidenhair ferns. Maidenhairs are distinguished by black stems and deeply dissected leaves, and are more tolerant of dry air than many of the other ferns. Long, broad fronds. Minimum temperature 55° F. *A. hispidulum* is a distinctive maidenhair from tropical Australasia. Its new fronds are copper pink.

Asplenium nidus

Family *Polypodiaceae*. Native to tropical Asia and Australia. Grows to 3 feet. Evergreen. Given room to develop, the bird's-nest fern is a magnificent plant with large, upright, translucent fronds of a distinctive pale green. It is semiepiphytic and can in fact be seen in the trees in the more humid parts of Oahu, Hawaii (as escaped plants, the spores having been distributed by the wind). Able to endure dry conditions at the roots for short periods. Minimum temperature 55° F.

Blechnum gibbum

Family *Blechnaeae* (*Polypodiaceae*). Native to New Caledonia. Its 3-foot trunk is topped by 3-foot fronds. Evergreen. This is a tree fern of close to manageable size for the greenhouse, for those willing to give over most of their space to shaded, humid conditions. A striking and distinguished plant with stiff, dark green, wide-spreading fronds. Avoid overhead watering. Minimum temperature 55° F.

Davallia fejeensis

Rabbit's-foot fern

Family *Davalliaceae*. Native to Fiji. Grows to 18 inches. Briefly deciduous in winter. A familiar house and greenhouse plant, it is beloved for its fuzzy creeping rhizome but also has attractive bright green, triangular fronds. Standard fern culture. The rhizomes can be used as cuttings for propagation. Minimum temperature 60° F.

Nephrolepis exaltata

Family *Oleandraceae*. Native to the tropics. Grows to 3 feet. Evergreen. Cultivar 'Bostoniensis' is the familiar Boston fern, a lush, majestic cascade of lacy fronds that is particularly good in a hanging basket. Subject to spider mites in a dry atmosphere, such as the interior of a house. Standard

fern culture. Minimum temperature 55° F. Another commonly grown species is *N. cordifolia*, the sword or ladder fern, which has a more upright habit of growth.

Platycerium bifurcatum (P. alcicorne)

Stag's-horn fern

Family *Polypodiaceae*. Native to Australia and Indonesia. Grows to 30 inches. Evergreen. A true epiphyte, grown in the house or greenhouse on slabs of bark or tree-fern stem, with a little compost inserted between the support and the base of the fern. Flat sterile fronds, green to begin with and aging to brown, anchor the fern to its support; the antler-like fertile fronds arch out into space. Water only when dry; otherwise, shade and high humidity. Can withstand 22° F. Offsets can be detached and grown on.

Fuchsia 'Voodoo'

Fuchsia 'Pink Cloud'

Polypodium aureum
Hare's-foot fern

Family *Polypodiaceae*. Native to Florida, South America, and Australia. Grows to 30 inches. Evergreen. The hare's-foot fern is not likely to be confused with the rabbit's-foot fern (*Davallia fejeensis*) since the leaves are entirely different and in fact quite unfernlike, with the individual fronds flat and broad and blue-green. There is a rhizome of hairy appearance, however. Standard fern culture, with particular emphasis on watering. Minimum temperature 50° F, but can withstand temperatures down to freezing and below. It is likely to lose its fronds temporarily if exposed to frost.

Fortunella

See *Citrus*

Freesia
Freesia

Family *Iridaceae*. Native to South Africa. Summer-dormant cormous perennials. Widely grown are a species and a hybrid:

F. × *kewensis* (*F. armstrongii* × *F. refracta*) and *F. refracta*   The hybrids are similar to the species but expand the color range of flowers from white to mauve, pink, red, yellow, and white. Grow to 12 inches. Flat, narrow leaves. Grown primarily for the color and fragrance of the spikes of flowers, which appear in late winter. The foliage itself is not so successful, flopping soon after appearing. However, if supported, as by a small hoop, it is neat and fresh-looking. Will prosper with no particular attention if grown in the ground; in pots needs restriction on summer moisture, although in most summers natural rainfall will not be excessive. Water and feed freely when in growth. Propagate by separating corms when dormant; can also be increased by seeds. Frost-tender (although the corms will survive) but prefers cool conditions, to 35° F, and needs them to flower well.

Fuchsia

Family *Onagraceae*. Native to tropical and temperate South America, New Zealand, and the Pacific Islands. Evergreen shrubs (under frost-free conditions) distinguished by pendant flowers of red, purple, pink, orange, and white in various mixtures, often in fancifully inflated shapes. Valuable for their graceful form, easy culture, and long period of bloom in summer and early fall. Some cultivars also have attractively variegated leaves. Some are well suited for hanging baskets. Standard culture with protection in summer from wind, dryness, and excess sun. Require some attention to shaping; cut back severely in spring then pinch out tip growth to induce bushiness. Attacked by spider mites and whiteflies; attractive to hummingbirds. Propagate by cuttings in spring.

F. × *hybrida*   A vast, varied array of hybrids, ranging in size from dainty basket types to vigorous shrubs that can reach 12 feet. Flower size, color, and degree of inflation are just as diverse; leaf color is almost as much so. Prefer cool winter temperatures, down to 32° F; light frost kills tender growth, but roots survive temperatures as low as 20° F. Among the many cultivars are 'Autumnal', good for red and gold leaves as well as rose and purple flowers; 'Baby Chang', a dwarf with small orange flowers; 'Cascade', an excellent basket type with lavender and white flowers; and 'Pink Cloud', with very large pink flowers that may come out even in winter in a warm greenhouse. 'Voodoo' is a proven performer of long standing. Its double plum-colored petals contrast with crimson sepals.

Gamolepsis chrysanthemoides

Gelsemium sempervirens

Gardenia jasminoides 'Veitchiana'

F. magellanica Native to southern South America. Grows to 3 feet when cut back by frost. A fuchsia for the coldest greenhouse, root-hardy to 0° F outside. Flowers are red and violet and very narrow, and are produced in profusion all along the stems.

Galanthus

See *Bulbs for Forcing*

Gamolepis

Family *Compositae*. One species is very valuable in the greenhouse:

G. chrysanthemoides Native to South Africa. Grows to 4 feet. Evergreen. A lusty, hardy shrub that is liberally covered with large, bright yellow flowers for much of the year. If anything can be said against it, it is that it is perhaps too vigorous, and yet it serves very well as a container plant, blooming when small and easily controlled by pruning. Pruning, in fact, is necessary to prevent a straggly

appearance. In the ground, it can readily fill an 8-foot bed. Standard culture; heat and drought resistant but looks better if well watered. Propagated by cuttings, which can be used for summer bedding. Hardy to somewhat below 32° F; even the flowers can withstand some frost.

Gardenia

Gardenia

Family *Rubiaceae*. Evergreen shrubs, of which one species is commonly grown in the greenhouse:

G. jasminoides (cape-jasmine; common gardenia) Native to South China. Glossy-leaved plants of great character, noted for the far-reaching sweet fragrance of the waxy white flowers that appear in summer and early fall. (Variety 'Veitchiana' is winter-flowering and requires higher temperatures than the typical

variety.) Can be good container plants but can also be touchy, dying suddenly for no clear reason. Standard culture with emphasis on summer watering and feeding; protect from sun and low humidity in dry areas. Need continuing attention to pruning weak or dead growth and removing spent flowers. Susceptible to spider mites, mealybugs, and aphids. Cultivars range in size from the 6-foot 'August Beauty' to the 6-inch 'Radicans' (also known as 'Prostrata'). Summer warmth is necessary for good flowering but they are tolerant of cold, down to 20° F, or 12° F for 'Radicans'. Propagate by cuttings in spring or summer.

Gasteria

See *Succulents*

Gelsemium

Family *Loganiaceae*. Native to the Deep South. Evergreen twiners, one of which is grown in the greenhouse:

G. sempervirens (Carolina-jasmine) Grows to 10

feet. A useful alternative to the more vigorous, more tender tropical vines; suitable for pot culture but at its best grown in the ground. Has long, lustrous leaves on a slender stem and very fragrant yellow flowers, borne from spring into summer. Winds its way up supports, casting only light shade. Standard culture; prune if the mass of foliage becomes too great on top. Propagate by cuttings. Hardy to 12° F. The plant is poisonous in all its parts if ingested.

Gerbera

Family *Compositae*. Native to Africa and southern Asia. Evergreen and deciduous herbaceous perennials. One species, with many selected forms, is widely grown in the greenhouse and as a bedding plant:

G. jamesonii (Barberton-daisy) Native to South Africa. Grows to 16 inches, with flower stems rising to 20 inches. Evergreen herbaceous

Aeschynanthus obconicus

Nematanthus gregarius

perennial. Invaluable for bright, dependable color. The large flowers, with colors ranging from cream through yellow and orange to red, appear at any time of year, with peaks in summer and late fall. They are long-lasting as cut flowers. Good as a container plant or in the ground. Standard culture, with attention to a rich growing medium, good drainage, and frequent feeding. Susceptible to mealybugs. Rapid grower, benefiting from division once it has become crowded. Dead leaves should be scrupulously removed. Propagate by division and by seeds. Fresh seed germinates readily and produces flowering plants in as little as 6 months under the best of conditions, but 18 months is more usual. Minimum temperature 32° F or somewhat less.

Gesneriads

Family *Gesneriaceae*. A large family filled with many exceptionally attractive evergreen houseplants, some of which will do well in a warm greenhouse that has a minimum temperature greater than 60° F and is shaded in summer. Even better summer treatment is to move the plants to an appropriate location outdoors. Gesneriads are mostly distinguished by evergreen leaves, in many cases distinctively attractive in themselves, and by their appealing, slightly asymmetric tubular flowers in a wide range of colors. Some are among the best of hanging plants. In addition to protection from direct sunlight, they need some care in watering; water only when the soil is dry, particularly in winter. Standard feeding and soil. Repot in spring. Propagated by seed and cuttings. Susceptible to mealybugs and whiteflies. Not always easy to grow, because they need good drainage yet are sensitive to drought.

Achimenes hybrids
Magicflower

Native to Central America. Deciduous; rhizomes dormant in winter. Grows to 10 to 20 inches. An abundance of bright, relatively large flowers on bushy or trailing plants. Store dry over winter; start into growth in spring with a minimum temperature of 60° F. 'Burnt Orange' is tall with orange flowers; 'Elke Michelssen' is compact with purplish pink flowers; 'Schneewitschen' is spreading with white flowers.

Aeschynanthus obconicus
Lipstick-plant

Native to Malaya. Reaches 12-inch spread. Good for hanging baskets. Thick, glossy leaves; bright red flowers borne profusely in winter.

Codonanthe aurora

Native to tropical America. Grows to 8-inch spread. Cascading habit makes it good for hanging baskets. Small, rose-pink flowers any time of year; small leaves with a satiny effect.

Columnea
Bonfire

Native to tropical America. Grows to 15-inch spread. Good for hanging baskets. Everblooming, with striking orange and yellow flowers and thick, shining leaves.

Kohleria 'Longwood'

Grows to 18 inches. Everblooming. Inflated flowers of crimson red speckled with cream carried well above the large, felted leaves. A vigorous, striking plant of upright, pyramidal form. Somewhat hardier than most gesneriads, it survives down to 35° F but performs better at a minimum temperature of 40° F.

Nematanthus gregarius (*Hypocyrta radicans*)

Native to Brazil. Grows to 18-inch spread. Good in hanging baskets. Excellent as a foliage plant, its thick leaves a dark, shining green. Yellow flowers, evocative of goldfish, are borne abundantly in winter.

Gesneriads

Gesneriads occupy a somewhat uneasy halfway position between houseplants and greenhouse plants, and are more of a challenge in either environment than might be expected. As a group, they do not like the extremes of heat, coolness, and light found in a greenhouse, but they want more light and much more humidity than a house is likely to provide. They are also quite susceptible to pests, particularly to mealybugs.

Nonetheless, they are well worth the challenge. All of the commonly grown gesneriads have exceptional flowers, often in the brightest of colors and often in the dead of winter; many also have outstanding foliage. Their shape as they grow can be very pleasing, and if conditions suit them they are very amenable container plants.

These are plants for center stage, and that is part of the problem, since center stage in the greenhouse is usually the hottest, brightest part. To be successful, gesneriads need a semishaded area. Given that, they will in general do well; only a too-low minimum temperature (less than 40° to 45° F, although there are noteworthy exceptions) will exclude them from the average greenhouse.

Kohleria 'Longwood'

Streptocarpus hybrid

Globba winitii

Haemanthus katharinae

Sinningia speciosa
Gloxinia

Native to Brazil. Grows to 8 inches. Deciduous; tuber dormant in winter. Bears spectacular large, bell-shaped flowers in summer in blue, violet, red, white, and shades in between. Minimum temperature 55° F. Plant tuber in spring, water sparingly until shoots appear, then water and feed regularly, taking care to keep water off the leaves. Dry off slowly after flowering is complete; store dry and not too cold over winter.

Smithiantha hybrids (Naegelia)

Native to Mexico. Grows to 10 inches. Plush-leaved plants with colorful flowers in shades of red, orange, pink, yellow, and white, in late summer and autumn. The season of bloom can be extended by potting up the dormant rhizomes at staggered intervals in late winter and early spring. Can withstand 35° F.

Streptocarpella 'Good Hope'
Native to South Africa. Grows to 8 inches. Good for hanging baskets. Provides an almost constant display of relatively large, light blue flowers. Small, fuzzy oval leaves.

Streptocarpus hybrids
Cape-primrose

Native to South Africa. Grows to 12 inches. Has long, slightly hairy leaves and large, African-violet–like flowers of blue, purple, pink, or white. Prefers more sun and drier conditions than other gesneriads. Propagated by leaf cuttings or seeds. Deteriorates after the first year or so.

Globba

Family *Zingiberaceae*. Native to tropical Asia. Evergreen perennials that spread by rhizomes. One species is particularly good for the greenhouse:

G. winitii (dancing-ladies)   Native to Thailand. Grows to 30 inches. Evergreen, but goes dormant in a cooler greenhouse. A creeping,

rhizomatous plant of delicate appearance with yellow tubular flowers enclosed in magenta bracts, borne in fall. Leaves are linear and sparsely borne on slender stems. Good in a pot or, in a larger greenhouse, as a loose, open ground cover. Standard culture. Propagate by division. Minimum temperature 40° F.

Gloriosa

Family *Liliaceae*. Native to tropical Africa and Asia. Deciduous. Grows to 3 to 6 feet. Restrained climber with magnificent flowers in summer. Normally grown in pots with supports provided for the twining tendrils. Leaves are solid and lance-shaped. Needs a warm greenhouse; minimum temperature 50° F. Provide copious moisture and feeding during the summer; gradually withhold water as the leaves begin to yellow in fall and store tubers dry and fairly cool (50° to 55° F) during winter. Repot in spring and water

sparingly until growth begins. Susceptible to mealybugs. Propagate by seeds and by division of the dormant tubers. The following species are native to tropical Africa:

G. rothschildiana (glory lily)   Large, wavy-edged flowers are brilliant red banded with yellow.

G. simplex   Orange-yellow flowers, slightly waved.

G. superba   Wavy flowers crimped along the edges, yellow aging to red.

Haemanthus

Family *Amaryllidaceae*. Native to southern Africa. Bulbous perennials with spring or summer dormancy. Broad, ribbed leaves are 1 to 2 feet long; large, showy umbels of small flowers are held well above the leaves. Standard culture when in growth; keep dry during period of dormancy. Pot up with the neck of the bulb just above the soil line, and water sparingly until growth begins. Withhold water when leaves begin to yellow. Best to leave in old soil for the next season, adding new soil to

Helichrysum petiolatum

Heliotropium arborescens

Hardenbergia violacea

the top or, after knocking root-ball from pot, the bottom. Minimum temperature 50° F, but 70° F is best when starting into growth. Attacked by snails and mealybugs. Propagate by removing offsets, or by fresh seed.

H. coccineus Very colorful; white anthers (tipped with yellow pollen) project from coral red flowers, the whole enclosed by scarlet bracts. Blooms in autumn before the leaves appear; keep thoroughly dry over the summer.

H. katharinae (bloodflower) Bright green, undulant leaves and large umbels of salmon red flowers; stamens are red. Blooms in summer.

Hardenbergia

Family *Leguminosae*. Native to Australia. Evergreen twining vines; among the best of vines for the greenhouse because of their relatively small size (to 10 feet), general toughness, and striking sprays of glowing violet flowers for a long period in fall and winter. Leathery, dark green leaves are carried sparsely. Standard culture; fairly drought resistant. Readily pruned; train onto a support or use as a ground cover. Propagate by summer cuttings or by seed.

H. comptoniana Delicate form to the foliage; leaves made up of lanceolate leaflets. Hardy to 24° F.

H. violacea A more robust look, with leaves like single lances. Also occurs in forms with white or rose flowers. Hardy to 20° F or below.

Haworthia

See *Succulents*

Helichrysum
Everlasting

Family *Compositae*. A widespread genus of annuals, perennials, and shrubs. Some have attractive, if subdued, flower heads. Those most valuable for the greenhouse have fragrant foliage which has the added advantage of emitting its fragrance when touched by the sun, not needing to be brushed or pinched. The foliage of many species is gray or even white, making them striking accents. Standard culture; very easygoing but must be trimmed for tidiness. Propagate by summer cuttings.

H. italicum (H. angustifolium, H. serotinum) (curryplant) Native to southern Europe. Grows to 1 to 2 feet. A dense, tangled pile of gray leaves without a hint of green; one of the best for scent. Insignificant yellow flowers. Hardy to 12° F.

H. petiolatum (licoriceplant) Native to South Africa. Grows to 1 foot tall by 4 feet wide. A large plant but readily kept to size by pruning; good in a hanging basket. Leaves are densely covered on both sides with a white felt marked with a darker pattern. Flowers are buff-white, but held prettily above the foliage. Hardy to 25° F.

H. psilolepis Native to South Africa. Grows to 6 inches and spreads. Has silvery, felted leaves; bright yellow flowers of substantial size are borne in summer. Good for hanging baskets.

Heliotropium

Family *Boraginaceae*. Annuals and shrubs widespread in tropical and warm-temperate regions. Of the many species, one has long been in greenhouse cultivation:

H. arborescens (H. peruvianum) (common heliotrope) Native to Peru. Grows to 6 feet. Evergreen shrub. Beloved for the intense fragrance of its lavender or white flowers. Flowers are borne in dense heads primarily in summer. Blooms when small; good container plant. Undistinguished form and foliage. Available varieties, differing in flower color, may not be equally fragrant. Propagate by seeds and cuttings. Minimum temperature 50° F.

Heterocentron

Family *Melastomataceae*. Native to tropical America. Shrubs and perennials. A single species is often grown in the greenhouse:

H. elegans (H. roseum, Heeria elegans, Schizocentron elegans) (Spanishshawl) Evergreen subshrub.

Hibiscus rosa-sinensis

Hibiscus rosa-sinensis 'Nagao 20'

Iboza riparia

Ixora javanica

Grows to 2 inches, with a spread of 2 feet or more. Bright-leaved creeper with rosy purple flowers spring through fall, peaking in summer. Delightful as a ground cover or in a hanging basket. Standard culture, but best in part sun or shade. Rapid grower but easily controlled. Propagate by cuttings or layers. Minimum temperature 40° F.

Hibiscus

Family *Malvaceae*. A large genus of ornamental annuals, perennials, and shrubs, only one of which is of interest for the greenhouse:

H. rosa-sinensis and hybrids (rose-of-China)   Native to tropical Asia. Evergreen shrub. Grows to 15 feet in nature; readily kept to 6 feet in a pot. Flaring hollyhock-like flowers in a range of vibrant colors—pink, red, white, yellow, and orange. Begins blooming when small, 2 feet or less. Extended period of bloom,

centering around late spring and early summer. Thrives in heat, otherwise standard culture. Protect from wind. Taller varieties become leggy without pruning; shaping is in general desirable for all varieties. Attacked by aphids. Propagate by cuttings; rooting is hastened if bottom heat is provided. Can take temperatures to 35° F.

'Agnes Galt': large pink flowers; vigorous and hardy.

'Cooperi': an old favorite, with variegated leaves and pink flowers.

'Fiesta': large orange flowers; vigorous and upright.

'Nagao 20': large blood-red flowers.

'Ross Estey': very large in foliage and flower, pink-tipped coral flowers.

'Ruth Wilcox': creamy white flowers with a rare hint of fragrance.

Hyacinthus

See *Bulbs for Forcing*

Iboza

Family *Labiatae*. A small genus. Only one cultivated species is known:

I. riparia   Native to South Africa. Evergreen perennial with a semiwoody stem. Grows to up to 4 feet. A delightful plant, willowy-stemmed with scalloped, fragrant leaves and long wands of white flowers in winter. Easily grown; standard culture with abundant water in summer, even to the extent of pool-margin conditions. Susceptible to mealybugs. Minimum temperature 45° F; frost-tender. Propagate by cuttings in spring or summer.

Iris

See *Bulbs for Forcing*

Ixora

Family *Rubiaceae*. Native throughout the tropics. Evergreen shrubs that bear large corymbs of bright flowers. Flowers appear at 18 to 24 inches, but in time the plants, with their large elliptical leaves and bushy growth, can become rather large for the greenhouse. Still, they can serve for many years as tub plants of stature and distinction. Standard culture, with particularly high humidity and a minimum temperature of 55° F. Propagate by cuttings.

I. coccinea (flame-of-the-woods)   Grows to 5 feet. Native to India. Flowers orange-red, but cultivars with flowers in various shades of pink and yellow also occur.

Jasminum officinale

Jasminum polyanthum

Ixora hybrids   Of uncertain parentage but clearly akin to *I. coccinea*, these hybrids often bear more heavily, and in a wide range of colors:

'Frances Perry': deep yellow flowers.

'Helen Dunaway': orange flowers.

'Henry Morat': pink flowers with some fragrance.

'Nancy Lee': flamingo pink flowers.

I. javanica (jungle-geranium)   Grows to 25 feet, but can be kept to 6 feet in a container for a long period. Flowers are salmon red.

Jasminum
Jasmine

Family *Oleaceae*. Native to tropical and warm-temperate regions of Asia, Africa, and Australia. A large genus of vines and vinelike shrubs, evergreen and deciduous. Quite large, 10 feet or more, but because of their lax, open growth that is amenable to pruning, they can readily be fit into the greenhouse. Some species are fragrant and some bloom in winter, but in general the two characteristics do not go together. Flowers are white or yellow; the famous fragrance is primarily restricted to the white ones. Plants tend to be untidy without rigorous pruning, but otherwise are attractive in foliage and flower. Standard culture. Somewhat susceptible to mealybugs. Propagate by cuttings.

J. humile   Native to the Himalayas. Evergreen. Usually seen as the variety *revolutum*. The rare exception, a fragrant yellow. Blooms in summer. Hardy to 20° F.

J. mesnyi   Native to China. Evergreen. A jasmine with some innate character of growth, forming a weeping top on relatively stout stems. Yellow flowers; blooms in winter. Hardy to 12° F, but the buds will freeze out at that low of a temperature, to be replaced by summer flowers.

J. nitidum (angel-wing jasmine)   Native to the southern Pacific. Evergreen. White flowers; blooms in summer; very fragrant. Distinguished by a purple cast to the buds and leathery, uncut leaves. Hardy to 25° F.

J. officinale (poet's jasmine)   Native from eastern Europe to western China. Deciduous in colder environments. White flowers; blooms in summer; fragrant. Easygoing; hardy to 12° F. *J. officinale grandiflorum* is smaller and hardier, with somewhat larger flowers.

J. parkeri   Native to China. Deciduous. A strange sort of jasmine—a small, compact, shapely shrub with scentless yellow flowers borne in May. An excellent container plant, or a useful garden subject for colder greenhouses. Hardy to 5° F under glass.

J. polyanthum   Native to China. Evergreen. Flowers are pink in the bud, then open to white. Blooms in summer; very fragrant. A strong grower but among the least hardy, being vulnerable to frost. Requires abundant sunlight.

Kalanchoe

See *Succulents*

Kohleria

See *Gesneriads*

Lachenalia bulbiferum

Lantana montevidensis

Laurentia fluviatilis

Lachenalia

Family *Liliaceae*. Native to South Africa. Bulbous, deciduous perennials with showy, pendant, tubular flowers in late winter or early spring. Leaves are broad and rather lax. Can endure house conditions readily if given good light; good for bringing inside when in bloom. Standard culture while in growth in winter; require dryness and protection from excessive heat during the summer dormancy period. Withhold water as the leaves yellow in late spring; renew watering when new growth shows in fall. Frost-tender, but survive down to the freezing point. Propagate by dividing the bulbs when dormant, and by seeds.

L. aloides (L. tricolor) (cape-cowslip) Stems reach 12 inches; leaves are as long but are carried near the ground. Flowers are yellow tipped with red on the inner segments, green on the outer.

L. aurea Grows to 12 inches. Golden yellow flowers. More difficult than the other species in its exacting demands for summer dryness.

L. bulbiferum (L. pendula) Stems reach 12 to 15 inches. Flowers are red and yellow, tipped with purple.

L. pustulata Grows to 8 inches. As implied by the somewhat unfortunate specific name, the leaves are patterned with projections, resulting in an attractive mottled appearance. Violet to blue flowers appear in March.

Laelia

See *Orchids*

Lampranthus

See *Succulents*

Lantana

Lantana

Family *Verbenaceae*. Native to tropical America. Floriferous evergreen shrubs. Leaves give off an odor when rubbed that is not universally appreciated. Fast growing; prune hard—very hard—to keep some semblance of shapeliness. Flowers, tightly packed in clusters, are borne continuously in a warm enough situation, otherwise primarily in summer. Good as hanging container plants and good for summer bedding. Standard culture with emphasis on exposure to sunlight; vulnerable to mildew in a shaded position. Allow soil to dry between waterings to encourage flowering. May be attacked by spider mites and mealybugs. Can endure some frost but does better at a minimum temperature of 45° to 50° F. Propagate by cuttings.

L. hybrida The plants usually seen in commerce; crosses between *L. camara* and *L. montevidensis*. Planted in the ground, they may spread to 6 feet, but are easily restricted to 2 to 3 feet in a pot.

'Carnival': relatively small; flowers pink, yellow, and crimson.

'Confetti': larger; flowers pink, purple, and yellow.

'Dwarf Yellow': relatively compact, flowers yellow.

'Radiation': flowers orange-red.

'Sunburst': flowers are bright yellow.

L. montevidensis (L. sellowiana) Available from some suppliers. Grows to up to 6 feet across. Rose-purple flowers.

Laurentia (Isotoma)

Family *Lobeliaceae*. A somewhat obscure genus that has provided one species well suited to greenhouse growing:

L. fluviatilis Native to Australia. A delightful, long-blooming ground cover, ½ inch tall, dotted with pale blue star flowers from late spring through summer, with a second flush in autumn. Evergreen, but deciduous in a subfreezing environment. Very good in pots. Excellent in the ground but, like most ground covers, vigorous enough to mound over and smother anything less than 5 inches high. A good companion plant for *Brachycome multiflora*. Standard culture with some tolerance for shade; will withstand foot traffic. Roots as it goes; propagate by detaching the rooted runners and treating them as newly rooted cuttings. Hardy to 5° F.

Leptospermum scoparium

Lithodora oleifolia

Leptospermum
Tea-tree

Family *Myrtaceae*. Native to Australia and New Zealand. Evergreen shrubs noteworthy for their small, shiny, tidy leaves and small, bright red, pink, or white flowers borne in abundance along the stems. Standard culture for young plants, with particular attention to good drainage; established plants are drought tolerant. The larger species grow large in nature (though blooming at a very small size) and require pruning to remain pot-sized. Frequent light pruning is best since old bare wood does not resprout. Propagate by cuttings and by seed.

L. humifusum Grows to 4 inches. Small, hardy, and highly drought tolerant, this is an excellent backbone plant for any type of greenhouse. White flowers are borne in early summer. Long shoots extend horizontally from the central stem but do not layer, forming a dense ground cover of shining leaves that is easily kept within precise limits. Somewhat slow growing but will cover a square foot in 2 or 3 years. Good in pots or in the ground. Hardy to 12° F.

L. scoparium Grows to up to 10 feet, but is readily kept much smaller in a pot. The most commonly grown *Leptospermum*, and well suited to pot culture; shapely in form whether upright or spreading. White, red, or pink flowers, depending on cultivar, in most cases are borne in spring. Hardy to 25° F. Cultivars include the following:

'Chapmanii': leaves tinged with bronze; rose flowers.

'Florepleno': compact; double pink flowers.

'Nanum': naturally small, grows to 1 foot; light pink flowers.

'Ruby Glow': one of the best; upright and vigorous; abundant red flowers in late winter and spring.

'Snow White': compact; double white flowers.

Leucadendron

See *Protea*

Ligularia

Family *Compositae*. A genus primarily composed of large, hardy, deciduous perennials, but one species is of interest for the greenhouse:

L. tussilaginea Native to the Far East. Evergreen. Grows to 3 to 4 feet. Grown almost entirely in the form of two variegated-leaf cultivars: 'Argentea' (cream and gray) and 'Aureomaculata' (leopardplant; green blotched with circles of yellow). An outstanding foliage plant that also bears a respectable head of yellow flowers in fall, held well above the leaves. A vigorous, rather large plant that can be kept to convenient pot size by yearly division. Standard culture, but suffers if exposed to excessive heat and light; benefits greatly from a summer outside. A good shade plant. Attacked by slugs and mealybugs; the latter are a constant menace in a warmer greenhouse. Retains foliage in good shape to 12° F under glass; root-hardy to 0° F. Is much easier to grow under cold conditions. Propagate by division as new growth starts in spring, giving the new plants extra shade and humidity for several weeks until well established.

Lithodora

Family *Boraginaceae*. Subshrubs and herbaceous perennials, one of which brings a quiet charm to the greenhouse:

L. oleifolia Native to the Mediterranean. Evergreen. Grows to 2 feet. A slow-growing shrub valuable for the soft blue flowers it bears in winter, as well as its compact growth and easygoing nature. A good container plant, one of the restrained company that is suitable for a group planting. Standard culture. Propagate by division.

Mandevilla × amabilis

Mandevilla sanderi

Mitriostigma axillare

Lobivia

See *Cactaceae*

Malpighia

Family *Malpighiaceae*. Native to tropical and subtropical America. Evergreen shrubs that serve well as foliage plants, having glossy, substantial leaves and good form; attractive clusters of small flowers are borne in summer. At least one species is important for its fruit. Standard culture. Propagate by seeds or cuttings.

M. coccigera (miniature holly) Grows to 3 feet. A shapely, upright bush, holly-like leaves and pink flowers.

M. glabra (Barbados-cherry) Grows to 10 feet. Slow-growing enough and flowering at a small enough size to serve as an attractive, distinctive container plant. Flowers in shades of pink or red are followed by small, sweet, juicy red fruits. Native as far north as southern Texas; northern forms have a fair degree of hardiness.

Mammillaria hahniana

See *Cactaceae*

Mandevilla

Family *Apocynaceae*. Native to the American tropics. Bold, vigorous evergreen and deciduous vines that produce an abundance of 3-inch-wide, funnel-shaped flowers in summer. They show to best advantage in a larger greenhouse, either in a large pot or in the ground, with sturdy supports for the stems. Standard culture, though may need shading in summer if kept under glass. Susceptible to spider mites. Propagate by cuttings.

M. × amabilis A hybrid of garden origin, this is the type most frequently grown. Grows to 10 feet but begins blooming when much smaller. Evergreen. Flowers open pink, mature to crimson. The flowers of cultivar 'Alice du Pont' remain a bright, glowing pink. Minimum temperature 40° to 45° F.

M. laxa; *M. suaveolens* (Chile-jasmine) Grows to 16 feet. Deciduous. Very fragrant white flowers. Root-hardy to 5° F. Unruly plants can be cut to the ground over winter and will bloom on new growth.

M. sanderi Grows to 6 feet. Evergreen. Bears light pink flowers over a long season; ever-blooming under warm enough conditions. 'Red Riding Hood' has very bright red flowers. Minimum temperature 32° F.

Matthiola incana

See *Annuals*

Miltonia

See *Orchids*

Mitriostigma

Family *Rubiaceae*. Native to South Africa. Evergreen shrubs. One species is commonly grown:

M. axillare (Gardenia citriodora) (wildcoffee) Grows to 5 feet. Closely enough related to the gardenia to have all its advantages— solid, glossy leaves and fragrant white flowers—but of somewhat easier culture. The scent of the flowers, which are borne in winter and spring, is reminiscent of orange blossoms. Good as a container plant; readily kept at a fraction of its size in the wild. Blooms while small. Standard culture. Susceptible to mealybugs. Propagate by cuttings.

Muscari

See *Bulbs for Forcing*

Narcissus papyraceus 'Paper White'

Ochna serrulata

Narcissus
Daffodil

Family *Amaryllidaceae*. Narcissus species and varieties are included under Bulbs for Forcing (see page 55), but one species that, in some of its forms, blooms particularly early merits its own heading:

N. bulbocodium (hoop-petticoat daffodil) Grows to 8 inches. Summer dormant. The hoop-petticoat daffodil is a charming species, but the variety 'Romieuxii' is of special interest to the greenhouse gardener. It comes from the mountains of Morocco and naturally blooms in the dead of winter between the middle of December and the end of January. It has the typical petticoat shape and is palest yellow. Two other varieties, *N. bulbocodium* var. *zaianicus lutescens* and *N. bulbocodium* 'Julia Jane', bloom somewhat later and are deeper yellow. Another excellent

white-flower type, *N. bulbocodium* 'Nylon', blooms in November and is more vigorous. The species seems to prefer container culture to growing in the ground, primarily because of its need for very good drainage. It needs good watering and feeding during its winter growth period and fairly dry conditions in summer. It is sufficient to leave the bulbs in the original pots and expose them to no more than natural rainfall. The appearance of green shoots in fall signals the time to resume watering. Hardy to 12° F or somewhat lower; colder conditions do not significantly affect the time of flowering, although blossoms may be damaged at the lowest temperatures. Propagate by dividing the dormant bulbs, and by seeds.

Nematanthus gregarius (Hypocyrta radicans)

See *Gesneriads*

Nemesia

See *Annuals*

Neoporteria chilensis

See *Cactaceae*

Nephrolepis exaltata

See *Ferns*

Ochna

Family *Ochnaceae*. Native to tropical and subtropical Africa and Asia. Evergreen trees and shrubs, one of which has come into greenhouse cultivation:

O. serrulata (O. multiflora) (Mickey-Mouse plant) Native to South Africa. Grows to 5 feet. Long,

crinkled oval leaves and pleasantly sinuous upright growth make this a handsome plant at any season, but the flowers and fruit are the real show. Fragrant yellow flowers appear in summer, developing into glossy black seeds surrounded by red sepals, suggesting the bright eyes and big ears of a mouse to a lively imagination. An easily grown container plant; slow-growing; flowers when fairly small, 18 to 24 inches. Standard culture with some shade from the full summer sun. Propagate by seed, best sown when fresh, and by cuttings. Minimum temperature 32° F or somewhat lower.

Opuntia

See *Cactaceae*

Cattleya BLC 'Cadmium Light'

Laelia autumalis

Orchids

Family *Orchidaceae*. Worldwide. Deciduous and evergreen herbaceous perennials. Orchids are among the best loved greenhouse plants for some very good reasons. First and foremost are the flowers, which stand out from those of any other family in their distinctive and often bizarre shapes and in their daring combinations of colors not otherwise seen in the plant kingdom. (The foliage of orchids is at best interesting, except in a few rare and difficult-to-grow cases where it is jewellike.) Second, the size of the plant is right. Seldom does an orchid outgrow all reasonable pots, although some cymbidiums may come close. Third, blooming time for many orchids is fall or winter. Fourth, they can be a challenge to grow and therefore a source of particular satisfaction. Fifth, their variety is endless, both in nature and in commerce.

These generalizations apply most strongly to one particular class of orchids, the aerial-growing or epiphytic ones. There are also terrestrial species whose culture is little different from any other garden plant, but they are much less showy and of less interest to the greenhouse grower.

The epiphytes themselves fall into three distinct classes (with some overlap) based on minimum temperature requirements: warm, 65° F (*Phalaenopsis, Vanda*); temperate, 55° F (*Cattleya, Dendrobium, Epidendrum, Laelia, Miltonia, Oncidium,* and mottled-leaf forms of *Paphiopedilum*); and cool, 45° F (*Cymbidium, Epidendrum, Laelia, Odontoglossum,* and green-leaf forms of *Paphiopedilum*). Other than minimum temperatures, however, their cultural requirements are very much the same.

The culture of epiphytic orchids is not difficult, just different, reflecting the very specialized niche that they have seized. In nature they grow in pockets of organic debris that accumulate in such places as the crotches of trees; folds, hollows, or rough spots in branches and trunks; and even rock faces. It is an environment that offers excellent drainage, frequent drought, and a slow, steady flow of nutrients from the breakdown of the debris plus the occasional bonanza of a dead insect. The typical epiphytic orchid is adapted to this environment with thick leaves and a waxy skin to reduce water loss; a pseudobulb to store water and nutrients; thick, exposed roots designed to hold fast to surfaces as well as absorb water and nutrients; and a need for a loose, fibrous, fast-draining medium. When translated to pot culture, this means that the orchid is less sensitive to drought than to overfeeding or poor drainage.

A proper medium comes first. Osmunda fiber was the medium of choice for a long time but has now been replaced in popularity by ground bark, which is readily available, inexpensive, and at least as effective. Pot or repot when new growth commences in the spring. Place the plant in a pot (severing roots that may be adhering to the old pot) and push the medium firmly around the remaining roots. Water then and at more or less weekly intervals while growth continues, gauging the timing by the lightness of the pot; feed with an orchid fertilizer every two weeks. The plant may do adequately without the supplemental feeding, but flowering will be less heavy and growth slower. Maintain high humidity but also provide good air circulation—these are plants of the upper, airier canopy. Many species require a well-defined rest period after the period of growth; in general, watering should be reduced and feeding stopped in fall and winter.

Cattleya 'Okami Mendenhall'

Cymbidium 'Sweetheart Lillian Reed'

Orchids need shading from the summer sun, particularly if kept inside the greenhouse. The amount of shading varies with the species.

Pests are normally not a problem, although there can be some infestation by mealybugs. Propagate by seed or by separation and potting up of divisions, both somewhat specialized techniques.

Cattleya

Native to tropical America. This genus, familiar to all for its large, colorful flowers that are a mainstay of corsages, is the familiar point of reference to which other genera are compared. Its culture is a model of general orchid culture, with its temperature and light requirements right in the middle of the range.

Cattleya is distinguished by thick, leathery, oblong leaves, a pronounced pseudobulb, and large flowers that can best be described as of typical orchid shape. It requires a 55° F minimum night temperature, and 5 to 10 degrees higher during the day; 50 to 60 percent humidity; and summer shading to reduce light to 40 percent of full intensity. Dark green, soft growth indicates too little light. Light intensity can be greater if air circulation is good. Flower colors and combinations range from the exquisite to the garish. The many cultivars and hybrids vary in plant size and frequency of flowering as well as color. With the rate of development of new varieties, it is certainly safest to see a plant in bloom before purchasing it. This applies equally to the other genera.

Cymbidium

Native to tropical Asia and Australia. Elongated, rather grasslike foliage and reduced pseudobulbs suggest a somewhat less obligatorily epiphytic nature, and indeed its culture is less demanding than many other genera. In addition, a relatively great tolerance of temperature extremes (32° to 85° F) makes it among the easiest of the orchids to grow. Requires stronger light than *Cattleya*. Flower range is not quite as extreme in the variety and combinations of colors, but the flowers are borne in large numbers on long stalks, resulting in a distinctive show. The major blooming period is from February to May, but some recent hybrids bloom into December.

Dendrobium

Native to tropical Australasia. Distinguished by long pseudobulbs that have the appearance of stems, and racemes of numerous flowers in a rich assortment of colors. Some species and the hybrids formed from them lose their leaves in winter and therefore have a pronounced need for a winter rest. Such requirements must be determined on a plant-by-plant basis. One of the easiest choices is *D. nobile* and its hybrids, which can be grown in the same way as *Cattleya* except under cooler, brighter, drier conditions in the winter. Clusters of pink to rose-purple flowers are borne in spring.

Epidendrum

Native to tropical America. Some species have a reedlike growth habit similar to *Dendrobium*; others have well-developed pseudobulbs more like those of *Cattleya*. The latter are more strictly epiphytic, can endure more sun and drought, and require a standard orchid medium. Some species, such as *E. cochleatum* (yellow-green sepals and petals, dark purple lip), are surprisingly hardy, able to endure 25° F for short periods. The reedlike types need less direct sun and more constant moisture, and are less fussy about medium. The most commonly available reed-stem hybrid is *E.* × *obrienianum*; its vivid red flowers rise a foot or so above the foliage.

Orchids

Who can explain the aura that surrounds orchids? A major part of their appeal is certainly that they dare to be different. Flower shape is one aspect of it; they offer every conceivable variation, bizarre and beautiful, on one clearly recognizable theme. Flower color may be even more significant. Nowhere else in the floral kingdom is there such a range of subtle, or gaudy, or clashing, or unique colors. All of this occurs against a backdrop of foliage that is best described as serviceable.

Orchids have a reputation for being difficult to grow, but that is more a hangover from the past than a present reality. Devising the proper growing medium is not the arcane art it once was, and a good deal is now known about the environmental requirements of many species. There has also been an on-going selection process for the easier hybrids, and tissue-culture propagation has made prices lower.

There is no good reason for a greenhouse gardener who likes orchids to be without them, although the cooler the greenhouse, the fewer the options. Yes, they will require some special effort, but that effort can be expended with every expectation of success.

Epidendrum

Cattleya hybrid

Laelia tenebrosa

Phalaenopsis

Miltonia

Vanda

Laelia

Native to tropical America. Very similar in appearance and culture to *Cattleya*, and in fact most widely developed in the form of the intergeneric hybrid, × *Laeliocattleya*.

Miltonia

Pansy orchid

Native to tropical America. Has well-developed pseudobulbs and clumps of long, arching leaves. Distinctive and endearing flowers are reminiscent of large, substantial, bright pansies, in blends of yellow, white, and red. Lowland and upland species differ in their needs for winter warmth, but all prefer cool shade in summer.

Odontoglossum species

Native to tropical America. Leaves and pseudobulbs similar to *Cattleya* in appearance, but the flowers are carried in great arching sprays. Typically from cool upland forests, therefore prefers cool conditions both winter and summer and shading from direct

summer sun. Many cultivars and hybrids have been developed, but one species, *O. grande*, the tiger orchid, is very popular and readily available and is typical of the genus. It has bright yellow flowers with rich brown stripes; they appear in the fall and last for three or four weeks.

Oncidium

Native from warm United States to tropical South America. Form of growth is similar to *Odontoglossum*, but the flowers in the sprays are generally smaller and more delicate; they are pleasant at a distance but require a close look to reveal their true excitement. Culture is like that of *Cattleya*. A good example is *O. papilio*, the butterfly orchid, whose flower parts (sepals, petals, and lip) are brown and yellow. Flowering can occur at any time of year, as new buds are continually forming.

Paphiopedilum

Lady's-slipper

Native to tropical Asia. Previously called *Cypripedium*, but that name is now reserved for the northern, hardy, deciduous lady's-slippers. The flowers are among the most appealing of the family although they come in a limited, rather muted range of green, white, or yellow, often with backgrounds of mahogany, tan, or maroon; they are glossy and look varnished. Flowers tend to appear one or two at a time. Requires more moisture than most other genera in winter, and can tolerate more shade. *P. insigne* is an easy introduction to the genus. Its sepals and petals have brown stripes on a green and white ground; the pouch is reddish brown. Coming from the Himalayas, it has some hardiness and can tolerate a few degrees of frost for brief periods.

Phalaenopsis

Moth orchid

Native to tropical Asia. Leaves are thick, pleated, and leathery; pseudobulbs are absent. The distinctively shaped

flowers are borne on short stems, generally no higher than the leaves. Very showy but somewhat more difficult to grow than the other genera. Requires a high minimum temperature (65° F) in winter and protection from extremes in summer, a good deal of shading, and constant moisture. The long-lasting flowers are borne in winter.

Vanda

Native to tropical Asia. Similar to *Phalaenopsis* in having no pseudobulb, but the leaves are either cylindrical or flattened. The leaves are attached to a stem that can become semiwoody and reach a formidable length, putting out heavy, tightly gripping aerial roots and requiring some type of support. Has some of the most unusual flower combinations in the family, exemplified by *V.* × *rothschildiana*'s strange shade of blue flowers with lighter stippling and dark veining. Light-loving even in winter, when strong light is necessary to induce bud set. Otherwise culture is similar to that of *Cattleya*.

Osmanthus fragrans

Oxalis regnellii hybrid

Osmanthus

Family *Oleaceae*. Widespread. Evergreen shrubs, including one of the best plants for the greenhouse:

O. fragrans (sweetolive) Native to China. Grows to 10 feet. An attractive, upright, slow-growing shrub of the easiest possible culture. Not noteworthy to look at even when in flower (which is all through the fall and winter), but the source during the blooming season of a searchingly sweet fragrance that comes and goes with the quirks of the greenhouse air currents. The flowers are small and white and nestled into the foliage; leaves are oval, leathery, and a dark glossy green. Very good in a pot despite its potential size; easily pruned, even sheared, but will make good growth if left to itself. Needs good light during the growing season. Because it is dormant in winter,

it can be brought into the house for extended periods, though the fragrance will fade somewhat after a week or so. Standard culture. Propagate by cuttings. Hardy to 12° F; flowers may be frost damaged but new ones will open. Another species, *O. heterophyllus* (*O. ilicifolius*), is sometimes grown, but it has irritatingly toothed holly leaves, is very shy to flower, and flowers in summer.

Oxalis

Family *Oxalidaceae*. Worldwide. Usually deciduous perennials, some of them bulbous, including species, such as *O. martiana (O. corymbosa)*, that are the most cheerily persistent pests the greenhouse can have; they spread by seeds and bulbils with the greatest abandon, choking out preferred plants or at least intruding on their effect. Others, however, are valuable container plants, with large, bright flowers and a restrained habit of growth. Culture varies somewhat

among the species, but all want a standard, well-draining medium and good light. Summer-dormant species do not need particular protection from moisture in the soil. New growth appears in early fall, at which time regular watering should begin. Propagation is primarily by division, and by seed if available.

O. brasiliensis Native to Brazil. Grows to 4 inches. Bulbous. Summer dormant. Wine red flowers in early spring over dense clumps of shiny, three-lobed leaves. Surprisingly hardy, surviving 0° F under glass.

O. lobata Native to Chile. Grows to 5 inches. Bulbous. Summer dormant. Yellow flowers are held well above the foliage for a long period in fall. Demands very good drainage. Hardy to 12° F.

O. purpurea; *O. variabilis* (grand-duchess oxalis) Native to South Africa. Grows to 6 inches. Bulbous. Summer dormant. Large flowers, pink to rose red, are borne fall to early winter. Easily grown; readily available.

O. regnellii Native to South America. Grows to 12 inches. Bulbous. Brief summer dormancy. One of the easiest to grow, flourishing in a sunny window with a minimum of care. Prefers to become dry between waterings. Attractive and distinctive, with strong stalks of white flowers and precisely triangular leaf segments.

O. versicolor (peppermint-stripe) Native to South Africa. Grows to 6 inches. Bulbous. Summer dormant. One of the best, with an abundance of flowers, white etched in red, fall through winter. Easily grown; becoming available. Hardy to about 20° F, but the flowers may be damaged.

Paphiopedilum

See *Orchids*

Parodia

See *Cactaceae*

Passiflora 'Incense'

Pelargonium × domesticum 'Mabel'

Pelargonium × domesticum

Passiflora
Passionflower, granadilla

Family *Passifloraceae*. Native to tropical and temperate Americas, with a few species from Asia. Grows to 20 to 30 feet. Vines, primarily evergreen, with large, spectacular, intricate flowers in shades of white, pink, red, and blue. Easily grown, even rampant; probably best grown in the ground, but some species bloom when small and are suitable as houseplants. Some bear edible fruit, which is not ready for eating until the skin is wrinkled and crackly. Standard culture. Provide support. Prune rigorously every year to keep plants open and untangled; this is particularly important because of their great susceptibility to mealybugs, which form large masses in hidden sections. Propagate by seeds and cuttings.

P. caerulea (blue passionflower; common passionflower) Native to Central America. Evergreen. Purple, white, and blue flowers in summer and autumn, followed by yellow fruits not described as edible. Hardy to 12° F; roothardy somewhat below that.

P. coccinea Native to South America. Evergreen. Showy crimson flowers with bright, protruding yellow stamens. Edible fruits are orange or yellow, striped with green.

P. 'Incense' Fragrant, wavy, royal purple flowers borne in summer. Hardy to at least 25° F.

P. quadrangularis (giant granadilla) Native to South America. One of the standard fruiting passionflowers. Very vigorous. Fragrant white, pink, or violet flowers in summer. Bears fruits 9 inches long, though hand-pollination may be necessary to produce them.

Pelargonium
Florist's geranium

Family *Geraniaceae*. Primarily from South Africa. Evergreen subshrubs. Living proof that familiarity does not always breed contempt, the hybrid pelargoniums remain the colorful mainstay of the greenhouse as well as the outside garden. They have many features to recommend them: large, bold clusters of flowers in shades and combinations of red, pink, white, and lavender; attractive, fragrant, often strikingly zoned leaves that can be used as herbs; shapely form (with pruning); and ease of culture as container plants. It is true that flowering time is in summer, but many cultivars continue to send out occasional blooms well into December. Standard culture, with a good deal of drought

tolerance, as suggested by the succulence of the stems. Does well in light shade. Prune as growth starts in spring. Remove spent flowers to encourage continuing bud production. Normally propagated by cuttings, but seeds produce different and possibly worthwhile types. Good in a cool greenhouse (minimum temperature 32° F) and will stand a few degrees of frost.

P. × domesticum (Martha Washington or regal geranium) Grows to 2½ feet. Most noteworthy for its flowers, which are individually large and come in a large range of striking colors, some brilliantly blotched. Leaves are dark green, solid looking, with crinkled margins.

P. × hortorum (common or zonal geranium) Grows to 3 feet, more if grown in the ground. Bears large clusters of flowers, most commonly in solid colors. Leaves large, flat, fragrant, sometimes banded with zones of different colors.

P. incrassatum See *Succulents*

Pentas 'Tu-tone'

Pentas 'California Lavender'

P. peltatum (ivy geranium)   Grows to 3 feet; trailing. Succulent, glossy, bright green leaves with a distinctively ivy cut. Flowers offer a good color range but are not as large as the above two. Good in hanging pots.

Pelargonium (scented leaves)   This category refers to the large number of species grown primarily for the sharp, evocative fragrances of their leaves. *P. crispum* smells like lemon; *P. graveolens* and others, like rose; *P. × nervosum*, like lime; *P. odoratissimum*, like apple. They bear flowers that would be considered quite satisfactory in another genus but pale beside their larger cousins. In general the plants are smaller, with smaller leaves, and are not quite as easygoing as larger geraniums, although if carefully grown they make striking container plants. If any one factor distinguishes their cultural needs, it is a greater sensitivity to over- or underwatering.

P. violareum (*P. tricolor*, *P. splendidum violare um*) Grows to 12 inches. A spreading subshrub with sprightly flowers that are red above and white or pale pink below, the two zones being very sharply defined. Heaviest bloom is in spring and summer. Good in a hanging pot.

Pentas

Family *Rubiaceae*. Native to tropical Africa. Evergreen shrubs, one of which is often grown in the greenhouse:

P. lanceolata (starcluster) Grows to 3 feet. A serviceable container plant. Attractive in foliage and flower, and easy to grow, but not of exceptional appearance. Flowers appear in large corymbs in matte hues of lilac, pink, or red in late summer and fall. Standard culture. Prune back as new growth begins in late winter. Minimum temperature 50° F. Propagate by cuttings.

Petunia

See *Annuals*

Phalaenopsis

See *Orchids*

Platycerium bifurcatum (P. alcicorne)

See *Ferns*

Polypodium aureum

See *Ferns*

Primula

See *Annuals*

Protea and Leucadendron

Family *Proteaceae*. Native to South Africa. Evergreen shrubs. Proteas and the closely related leucadendrons are famed for their flowers, so large that it would seem only a tree could carry them. In fact, most species are not of great

size: 3 to 5 feet tall and spreading as much. They are also distinctive for their twisting stems and thick, broad, tough leaves. The flowers are very colorful as well as large, with great variation from one plant to another within a species. Flowers in summer.

There are many species, most with finicky requirements, but several are easy enough and small enough to merit the challenge of seeking them out. By and large they are available only by seed (though cuttings root fairly readily if a parent plant can be found), and the seed is most dependable if from a source in South Africa itself. Plants are likely to take 5 years or more from seed to bloom. The species described here respond to standard culture and do well as container plants. They have very little hardiness, not surviving below about 25° F.

Punica granatum 'Chico'

Punica granatum 'Wonderful'

P. burchellii (*P. pulchra*) Grows to 3 feet. Upright stems on a spreading plant; leaves are hairy. One of the easiest to flower; flowers in subdued shades of pink and lavender.

P. cynaroides (king protea) Grows to 2½ feet. A tough, adaptable plant with some of the most spectacular flowers of the genus, in a variety of colors arranged in bands; a mainstay of the cut-flower industry. Roundish, smooth leaves; decumbent stems.

P. speciosa Grows to 3 feet. Another sturdy grower, upright, with somewhat hairy leaves. Perhaps the easiest to grow from seed.

Leucadendron daphnoides Grows to 3 feet. The members of this genus tend to be more difficult to grow than the proteas, but this species does well in a pot. It has a lax habit of growth. The flowers are cone-shaped and not as large as the typical protea flower; they are yellow and are borne in winter.

Psidium
Guava

Family *Myrtaceae*. Native to tropical America. Evergreen shrubs that bear edible fruit. Attractive, shiny green leaves; single-stemmed, branching growth. Small white flowers in summer. Adaptable, ornamental container plants. Standard culture. Respond to pruning. Propagate by cuttings or seed, although seed will lead to plants of uncertain performance. About 5 years from seed to flowering and fruiting. (For pineapple guava, see *Feijoa*, page 72.)

P. cattleianum (*P. littorale*) Grows to 9 feet. Two flavors, lemon (yellow fruit) and strawberry guava (red fruit). If any fruit bearer challenges *Citrus* as a greenhouse plant, it is this one. It is a plant of relatively small size at fruiting (4 feet), easy culture, and distinctive and tasty fruit that is unavailable in the

north. Able to tolerate a few degrees of frost and does well at a minimum temperature of 32° F, but probably performs best under somewhat warmer conditions.

P. guajava (guava) Grows to 20 feet. Although this is the more familiar of the guavas, it is on several counts less suitable for greenhouse growing. It is taller, less hardy, and bears fruit that is considered by some to be inferior.

Punica

Family *Punicaceae*. Native to Eurasia. Deciduous shrubs, one of which is often grown in the greenhouse:

P. granatum (pomegranate) Grows to 10 feet. One of the few leaf-losing (in winter) woody plants included here, it has a special role in a greenhouse garden that emphasizes seasonal displays. Good upright form. The leaves, when they appear in the spring, are copper colored, changing to

shiny green. In fall they are bright yellow. Brilliant orange-red flowers are borne in the summer, followed in some varieties by the large, leathery-skinned, tart and seedy fruits. Standard culture, but very tolerant of heat, drought, and alkalinity. Susceptible to mealybugs. Propagate by cuttings. Most forms sold are named cultivars so will not come true from seed, but seed will germinate readily and, of course, is readily available. Cultivars include 'Wonderful' for fruit, and 'Chico' and 'Nana' for low-growing, compact container plants, but not edible fruit. Hardy to 20° F, 'Nana' to 12° F.

Rebutia

See *Cactaceae*

Reinwardtia indica

Ruellia macrantha

Ruellia makoyana

Reinwardtia

Family *Linaceae*. Native to southern Asia. Two species of evergreen subshrubs, one of which is proving to be a valuable greenhouse plant:

R. indica (yellowflax) Grows to 3 feet. A very amenable container plant. Bears large, glowing yellow flowers right through fall and winter; each flower lasts only a day or two but is promptly replaced. Foliage and form are pleasant but undistinguished. Standard culture. Improved by pruning in spring; a common strategy is to use the trimmings as cuttings and to discard the parent plant after it has had two or three seasons of bloom. However, it also can be used as an in-ground accent or tall ground cover, where it will spread by underground stems, that can be lifted and divided. Minimum temperature 40° F.

Rhipsalis paradoxa

See *Cactaceae*

Rosmarinus

Family *Labiatae*. Native to the Mediterranean. One evergreen shrub is invaluable for the greenhouse:

R. officinalis (rosemary) Grows to 3 feet. One of the basic greenhouse plants, and the most suitable and useful herb for greenhouse culture. An attractive foliage plant, with upright, twisting, picturesque stems and fragrant needle leaves that are always available for cookery. Pale to dark blue flowers are small and, in a warmer greenhouse, sporadic, but they appear regularly through the winter in a subfreezing one. Good as a container plant or in the ground. A variety such as 'Tuscan Blue' can even be pressed into service as a Christmas tree. Standard culture; can tolerate extremes of cold and heat. Can be pruned to achieve a desired shape but is attractive if left to its own devices. Propagate by cuttings. Hardy to 12° F.

'Albiflorus': white flowers.

'Collingwood Ingram' (which may be the same as 'Benenden Blue'): strong blue-violet flowers.

'Prostratus': an eccentric trailer, considered by some to be a separate species, *R. lavandulaceum*.

'Tuscan Blue': an upright grower to 6 feet, with dark blue-violet flowers.

Ruellia

Family *Acanthaceae*. Native primarily to tropical America. Evergreen perennials or subshrubs. Easy, rewarding plants for the warmer greenhouse, with showy tubular flowers held on stalks above attractive dense, spreading foliage. Usually grown as pot plants but also serve well as ground covers. Standard culture. Minimum temperature 50° F to ensure good bud set. Propagate by cuttings and seed, or division if grown in the ground. Often grown on as cuttings (which bloom when 6 to 8 inches tall); the parent plant is frequently discarded after a year or two of bloom, but older plants remain attractive if pruned back after flowering.

R. graecizans (R. amoena) Grows to 2 feet high; spreads to 3 feet. Bright red flowers sent up from the axils of the leaves.

R. macrantha (Christmas-pride) Grows to 5 feet. The most widely grown *Ruellia*, prized for its rosy purple flowers carried for much of the year, particularly in winter.

R. makoyana (monkey-plant) Grows to 1½ feet. As much a foliage as a flowering plant, with soft, plushy leaves vividly veined white, and carmine flowers.

Salvia coccinea

Salvia leucantha

Salvia
Sage

Family *Labiatae*. Worldwide. A large genus with members to fit every situation. Some with bold spikes of bright flowers and fragrant foliage are worthwhile for the greenhouse, but all tread close to the borderline of weediness. Easily grown and adaptable in use, salvia does equally well in pots and in the ground in a wide range of temperatures. Standard culture. Susceptible to aphids. Propagate by cuttings or division; can also be propagated by seed if the other methods are not possible.

S. clevelandii Native to California. Evergreen shrub. Grows to 4 feet. A good container plant or a distinguished accent in a larger greenhouse. Has smooth, tidy gray-green leaves; bears blue flowers in summer. Admirably suited to greenhouse growing, being comfortable with high temperatures and very little moisture in summer; needs more moisture in winter. Otherwise standard culture. Blooms when 12 inches high. Hardy to 20° F.

S. coccinea Native to the American South. Evergreen subshrub. Grows to 2 feet. Valuable for the bright red flowers it bears in autumn. The flower-to-foliage ratio is relatively small, however, and the plant can be on the rampant side. Hardy to 20° F.

S. guaranitica Native to Central America. Evergreen subshrub. Grows to 3 feet. Less well known but desirable for the cobalt blue flowers it carries in fall and winter.

S. leucantha (Mexican-bush sage) Grows to 4 feet. Evergreen. A striking plant for pots or in the ground. The flowers are small and white but are surrounded by showy purple or rose calyces in summer and fall and into winter. Stems are upright, graceful, and slightly arched. Standard culture but drought tolerant. Blooms at 6 inches. Cut older stems to the base in spring, particularly if the plant is grown in the ground. Hardy to 25° F, but flowers and leaves may be damaged by frost.

S. splendens See *Annuals*

Schlumbergera bridgesii
See *Cactaceae*

Scilla
See *Bulbs for Forcing*

Scutellaria
Family *Labiatae*. Worldwide. Two evergreen subshrubs are of interest for the greenhouse. Showy fountains of flowers rise above the heavily veined leaves. These are container plants of long standing; they bloom when small. Standard culture. Minimum temperature 55° F. Propagate by seeds or cuttings.

S. costaricana Grows to 3 feet. Yellow-tipped tubular red flowers are borne most heavily in summer but appear throughout the year.

S. javanica Grows to 18 inches. Flowers are bright blue, spring through fall.

Sedum
See *Succulents*

Selenicereus grandiflorus
See *Cactaceae*

Serissa
Family *Rubiaceae*. Native to Southeast Asia. There is a single member of the genus:

S. foetida (*S. japonica*) Grows to 2 feet. Evergreen shrub. There is nothing very distinctive about this plant, but it is quietly pleasant in all its parts. It is easily grown, readily available, and adaptable to a number of uses. Small, glossy, sometimes variegated leaves are held on thin, wiry stems. Form is upright, branching and open; flowers are small, white, sparse, and borne through much of the year. Excellent for instant bonsai or any type of pot growing; amenable to shaping and pruning. Standard culture. Propagate by cuttings. Hardy to 20° F.

Scutellaria costaricana

Vallota speciosa

Sinningia speciosa

See *Gesneriads*

Smithiantha hybrids

See *Gesneriads*

South African Bulbs

South Africa is a rich source of valuable greenhouse plants. There are far too many worthwhile species of bulbous South African plants to list them all here. Instead, this is a sampling of plants that share a common effect—they are upright growers with 1- to 2-foot-long linear, swordlike leaves topped by stalks of showy flowers. They are excellent container plants. (*Babiana*, described on page 50, has a different impact and use because it is smaller.) They thrive under standard conditions of light and soil; watering and feeding vary depending on whether a species is summer dormant, winter dormant, or evergreen. Propagation is by division of the bulbs (or tubers, corms, or rhizomes) and by seed.

Ixia

Family *Iridaceae*. Most often grown are the hybrids, which come in a range of colors— white, orange, yellow, red, pink, and purple. Blooms April to June. Tolerates normal rainfall when dormant in summer. Minimum temperature 32° F.

Nerine

Family *Amaryllidaceae*. Valued for its toughness and late season bloom. Summer dormant, though *N. bowdenii* will send up leaves in summer if grown in a subfreezing greenhouse. Hardy to 25° F except *N. bowdenii*, which is hardy to 12° F.

N. bowdenii: pink flower; blooms October to November.

N. flexuosa: pink or white flowers; blooms in fall.

N. sarniensis (Guernsey-lily): brilliant vermillion flowers; blooms in fall.

N. undulata (*N. crispa*): pink flowers; blooms September to October.

Schizostylis coccinea

Family *Iridaceae*. Crimson flowers are borne October to November. Variety 'Mrs. Hegarty' bears rose pink flowers. Hardy to 20° F, but evergreen foliage may suffer.

Sparaxis hybrids

Family *Iridaceae*. Closely related and similar to *Ixia* except flowers tend to be splashed with strongly contrasting colors and appear earlier in spring. Summer dormant. Minimum temperature 32° F.

Tulbaghia

Family *Alliaceae*. Closely related to onions, these emit an odor of garlic when the leaves are bruised. Evergreen, though they may lose leaves if exposed to prolonged subfreezing conditions. Will endure temperatures to 20° F.

T. fragrans has broad gray-green leaves and bears fragrant lavender flowers in winter.

T. violacea (society-garlic) has narrower, blue-tinted leaves and bears its flowers primarily in summer, although some may appear at other times of year.

Vallota speciosa

Scarboro-lily

Family *Amaryllidaceae*. Evergreen. Easy and vigorous. Brilliant red-orange flowers borne in summer and early fall. Minimum temperature 32° F.

Veltheimia bracteata; V. undulata; V. viridifolia

Family *Liliaceae*. Has broad, attractive, wavy-margined leaves. Pale rose flowers tipped with green in long spikes are borne winter to early spring. Can be grown as

South African Bulbs

South Africa represents one of the great treasure chests for the greenhouse gardener, one that has only been dipped into but has already yielded spectacular results. The treasure, however, is not always easily won. Many species have very narrow requirements, a result of the crazy quilt of climates that characterizes the area, where summer-wet and summer-dry regions exist practically side by side. Soil, watering, and feeding all have to be mastered for these plants to be grown in the greenhouse.

The bulbous species of South African plants have proven most growable. They are not necessarily more adaptable than other plants from the region, since in many cases they do have strict requirements, but their requirements are well known and easily provided for in a greenhouse. Here at last are plants that fully appreciate the hot, dry conditions of the greenhouse in summer.

The plants are available not just as seeds but as dormant bulbs or tubers, and from domestic suppliers at that. They are colorful and distinctive, and should be an inducement to try more of the riches of the region.

Tulbaghia violacea

Velthemia viridifolia

Haemanthus katharinae

Strelitzia reginae

Crassula turgida (front) and *C. schmidtii*

an evergreen but may benefit from a drying off in summer. Minimum temperature 40° F.

Watsonia

Family *Iridaceae.* Particularly stately in effect, the leaves reaching 2½ feet and forming a well-shaped fan.

W. beatricis: Evergreen; orange-red flowers in late summer to fall.

W. marginata: Winter dormant; fragrant rose-pink flowers in early summer.

Stapelia

See *Succulents*

Strelitzia

Family *Strelitziaceae.* Native to southern Africa. Large evergreen perennials, one of which is grown in the greenhouse:

S. reginae (bird-of-paradise) Grows to 5 feet. Few plants are more aptly named. Its flower almost outdoes its namesake in brilliant

blue and orange plumage, and bears an uncanny resemblance to the head and beak of a bird. It is a large plant with tall, ribbed, paddle-shaped leaves of a leathery texture. It can be something of a spreading menace if planted in the ground. However, it serves well as a pot (or tub) plant, although it cannot be expected to bloom until it has filled a 10- or 12-inch pot, which takes 3 or 4 years from seed. Flowers can appear at any time, but the peak seasons are spring and fall. Sometimes sets seed. Standard culture; easily grown but susceptible to mealybugs, which can get out of hand in the dense growth. Propagate by division as well as by seed. Minimum temperature 45° F.

Streptocarpella

See *Gesneriads*

Streptocarpus hybrids

See *Gesneriads*

Strobilanthes

Family *Acanthaceae.* Native to tropical Asia. Evergreen bushy perennials with attractive leaves and flowers. They make good, striking container plants even when small. Standard culture. Mature plants need pruning for shapeliness. Propagate by cuttings.

S. dyeranus (Persianshield) Grows to 2 feet. The foliage is outstanding—tints of green and silver on an iridescent purple background. The flowers, borne in spikes at the ends of the stem, are pale blue or lavender. They appear primarily in winter. Minimum temperature 55° F.

S. isophyllus Grows to 2½ feet. Leaves are dark glossy green and willowlike; darker lavender flowers appear throughout the winter. Minimum temperature 32° F.

Succulents

Plant species from many different families have evolved adaptations to life in arid regions. In most cases they share a distinct, well-defined set of cultural requirements: They need full sun, excellent drainage, and lean soil. They require very dry conditions in winter, when they are dormant; in summer they need as much watering as nonsucculents, but with an emphasis on good drainage. For the best flowering, they need fertilizer high in phosphorus applied at frequent intervals. *Evergreen* can be an ambiguous term when applied to succulents (many succulents do not have true leaves), but it is safe to say that those included here are not leaf-losing. Drought tolerant, slow growing, and often naturally small, succulents are well suited for pot culture. Within the greenhouse, their specialized cultural requirements tend to lead to grouping succulents together; so do their often bizarre shapes, which do not always mix well with other types of plants.

Succulents

Succulents come in all shapes and sizes, with or without leaves, herbaceous or woody. One generalization can safely be made, however: They all have at least one part—stem, root, or leaf—that is swollen with stored water. That is the definition of a succulent.

Otherwise, generalizations fail. Many different genera have produced xerophytic species—species adapted to dry or hot and dry climates. In some, such as *Pelargonium,* succulent species retain many physical similarities to the nonadapted species. In others, such as *Euphorbia,* the succulents look nothing like the parent stock; in fact, they look confoundingly like a totally distinct group, the cacti.

A few succulents have exacting cultural requirements, but most are easygoing. Those that are commonly available are amenable, rewarding greenhouse plants, always arresting in form and often beauti-

Haworthia retusa

ful in flower. Some do so well they may become weeds, since they can reproduce from the tiniest crumb of a broken-off leaf. Even then, they are appealing and are among the most tolerated greenhouse pests.

Kalanchoe tubiflora

Crassula simsii

Adenium obesum

Aeonium tabuliforme

Their drought tolerance extends as well to dryness of the atmosphere, and for this reason more than any other they are useful as houseplants. In a house, however, their growth is likely to be at a standstill, if not in fact in a slow decline. In a greenhouse they find conditions enough like those of their native habitat that they can develop as they should. They will prosper enough to flower, often a spectacular event. Although very well adapted to endure low humidity, they also are able to handle the fairly high levels (70 percent or so) in a cool greenhouse over winter.

Succulents are among the limited group of plants that can tolerate the aridity and heat of a greenhouse in summer, as long as they are copiously supplied with water. Cold tolerance is more variable. Many cacti can withstand some frost, but in other families most species are tender. Exceptions are noted in individual entries.

A few succulents bear edible fruit. An especially good example is *Opuntia ficus-indica*, pricklypear. Seeds, acquired perhaps from a supermarket fruit, readily and quickly yield a vigorous plant. The plant, however, is quite large and ungainly for the greenhouse.

Most succulents are easily raised from seed (although the seedlings often remain small for the first year), from cuttings and layers, and by grafting. Cuttings need to be exposed to the air first to allow a callus to form on the cut surface (without which they are very likely to rot). Then place them on or slightly in a bed of barely moistened sand and keep them in a warm, shaded spot. They should not be enclosed.

Most succulents are seriously vulnerable to mealybugs and less so to other pests.

The number of succulent species suitable for a greenhouse is immense, but in attractiveness and ease of culture some species are a good deal more suitable than others. Among the more commonly grown genera, many of the favorites are cacti (*Cactaceae*), which, being too numerous to include here, are listed separately on page 57.

Adenium

Family *Apocynaceae*. Native to tropical Africa. Evergreen when cultivated. Grows to 6 feet, but is very slow growing and blooms when small. The species commonly grown is *A. obesum* (desertrose). It is notable for its swollen caudex, or basal stem, which quickly tapers into a stem of normal proportions that is topped by a globe of foliage—a symmetrical and pleasing arrangement. Glowing-pink flowers are borne freely in summer; leaves are a lustrous green. Propagate by seeds and cuttings.

Aeonium

Family *Crassulaceae*. Native to the Mediterranean region and the Canary Islands. Evergreen herbs or subshrubs distinguished by large rosettes of leaves in precise geometrical patterns. Individual rosettes die once flowering is completed, which means the end of the plant in those species that grow as a single rosette rather than as a cluster.

A. arboreum 'Atropurpureum' (blacktree) grows to 3 feet and has dark purple leaves and a sparsely branched, treelike shape. It bears panicles of yellow flowers in winter, and survives the experience.

A. tabuliforme, a particularly striking species with a rosette up to 20 inches across, flowers only once. It also has yellow flowers. As with other species, it can be kept going with leaf cuttings and initiated with seeds.

Echeveria glauca

Euphorbia candelabrum

Aloe

Family *Liliaceae*. Native to Africa. Evergreen succulents with fleshy leaves in geometric array. Many species are large and treelike, but a number of others begin flowering at a small enough size to serve well as container plants, and in fact are unusually attractive even when not in flower. At a large size they may be somewhat awkward because of the sharp teeth that edge the leaves. Frost-tender; most do best above 40° F, although they will survive down to 32° F. Easily grown from seed; reach flowering size in four to five years.

A. affinis Grows to 3 feet. Bears orange-red flowers in November above fleshy, heavily toothed leaves. Hardy to 28° F.

A. aristata Grows to 4 inches. One of the most commonly available aloes, and one of the smallest. Has dark green leaves with white spines; bears orange-red flowers in summer.

A. barbadensis (*A. vera*) Not the choicest of the genus but perhaps the best known. Familiar to many as the "burn plant"; the juice is considered useful for treating burns and other skin irritations. Pendulous growth to 2 feet, making a mature plant difficult to place. Yellow flowers are rarely produced.

A. rauhii Grows to 4 inches. Has gray-green, mottled leaves and racemes of rose flowers.

Cactaceae

Cacti
See page 57

Crassula

The type genus of the family *Crassulaceae*, and filled with excellent plants for the greenhouse. They have thick, succulent leaves that are either flat or beadlike.

C. argentea (jadeplant) Native to southern Africa. Omnipresent because it is highly individual and easygoing. In the greenhouse it will grow to specimen size, 3 feet or larger, and will bear white or pink flowers.

C. falcata Native to southern Africa. Long, flattened, gray-green leaves and bright orange-red flowers that are unusually showy for the genus. It can reach 3 feet.

C. schmidtii and *C. simsii* Native to southern Africa. A special pair, both low growing (4 to 6 inches), well mannered, fall and winter blooming, and hardy to 20° F. In appearance they are quite different.

C. schmidtii has long, tapered, thick leaves topped by clusters of pinkish flowers.

C. simsii is a mat of square rosettes dotted with tiny white flowers.

C. turgida (pagoda village) has tiered triangular leaves that suggest a hillside village. It grows to 10 inches and bears white flowers in abundance.

Drosanthemum

Family *Aizoaceae*. Native to South Africa. Evergreen mats good as easy-care, long-blooming ground covers.

D. floribundum has small cylindrical leaves and pale pink asterlike flowers in summer.

Echeveria

Family *Crassulaceae*. Native to the Americas. Quite a bit like crassulas but with more generally noteworthy flowers and a more pronounced tendency to grow in compact clusters.

E. agavoides (wax-agave) forms beautifully symmetrical 9-inch rosettes of green leaves tipped with red, above which rises a 20-inch stalk topped with reddish flowers.

E. glauca (*E. secunda glauca*) forms rosettes of leaves with a pronounced blue-gray cast. It grows to 3 inches and bears red flowers in racemes in spring and summer.

Euphorbia

Family *Euphorbiaceae*. Species listed native to South Africa. The succulent euphorbias contain some look-alikes to the cacti (which are restricted to the Americas), inhabiting similar environments in South Africa. The best clue to identity is internal—euphorbias exude a milky, sometimes caustic sap when cut.

Lampranthus aureus

Stapelia gigantea

E. grandicornis (cow's-horn), with its flat pads tipped with spines, mimics the *Opuntia* type of cactus. It reaches 3 feet and bears clusters of small yellow flowers.

E. obesa looks uncannily like a barrel cactus but without the thorns. It reaches 8 inches; its flowers are insignificant.

E. candelabrum is multi-branched and upright. The form 'Varigatum' has an overlay of creamy white.

Gasteria

Family *Liliaceae*. Native to South Africa. Fine small plants with long fleshy leaves and showy flowers.

G. caespitosa (pencilleaf), grows to 5 inches and bears pink flowers in late winter.

G. liliputana, even smaller at 2 inches, has chocolate-blotched leaves and red flowers.

Haworthia

Family *Liliaceae*. Native to South Africa. Low-growing plants grown for their foliage. Fleshy triangular leaves grow in a tight clump.

H. fasciata (zebra haworthia), 4 inches across, is one of the most commonly grown. Its leaves are a shining green marked out with lines of large white tubercles.

Kalanchoe

Family *Crassulaceae*. Native to Africa and Asia. Quite like the crassulas but distinguished by truly showy flowers. The foliage is also outstanding in some cases.

K. manginii is good in a hanging basket. It has shiny green leaves and bears balloonlike orange-red flowers in late winter.

K. pumila offers one of the best combinations of foliage and flowers—silver gray leaves and soft pink blossoms. It grows to 12 inches. Both are from Malagasy and need a minimum temperature of 45° F.

K. tubiflora (chandelier plant), also from Malagasy, grows to 3 feet. It has a single stem with few branches, and bears scarlet flowers. Its leaves develop plantlets at their ends that can be removed and potted up.

Lampranthus

Family *Aizoaceae*. Native to South Africa. Another large family filled with succulent ground covers that are excellent for the greenhouse.

L. aureus forms a low, dense bush of thick cylindrical leaves; it grows to 16 inches. In late winter it is covered with large, many-rayed flowers of a particularly beautiful golden orange.

Pelargonium

Family *Geraniaceae*. Most species native to South Africa. The succulent pelargoniums are more difficult to obtain and somewhat harder to grow than the familiar vigorous florist's types (see page 92), but they are just as valuable in the greenhouse. There are a number of species that are true xerophytes (lovers of dryness); one of the best, *P. incrassatum*, forms a mound of deeply cut, fleshy leaves, from which a spike of relatively large deep red flowers emerges in summer. Grows to 6 inches.

Sedum

Family *Crassulaceae*. This large genus includes many hardy species familiar to rock gardeners. Others are tender and more appropriate to greenhouse growing.

S. morganianum (donkey's-tail)   Native to Mexico. Grows to 2 feet. Thick, fleshy, silver blue elliptical leaves are arranged neatly along decumbent stems that sport purple flowers in spring.

S. × rubrotinctum (jellybeans)   Native to Mexico. Grows to 8 inches. Rosy-tipped, bean-shaped leaves grow on upright stems. Yellow flowers bloom in late winter.

Stapelia

Carrionplant

Family *Asclepiadaceae*. Native to South Africa. A genus distinguished by flowers that are overwhelming in size, lurid colors, and odor; their rotting-meat smell suits the flies that pollinate them. They have fleshy, angular stems forming well-shaped upright or decumbent plants. Minimum temperature 45° F.

Swainsona galegifolia

Thunbergia grandiflora

Tibouchina urvilleana

S. gigantea (giant toadplant) has flowers that are large even for the genus; they are yellow with red ridges. Grows to 12 inches.

S. nobilis has flowers of a darker yellow with a thicker purple pile.

Swainsona

Family *Leguminosae*. Native to Australia. Evergreen shrubs, one of which is grown in the greenhouse:

S. galegifolia (Darling River pea)   Grows to 4 feet. A lax shrub best treated as a vine, with some type of support. An ornamental container plant at all times, with loose, open growth and slender pinnate leaves. Showy racemes of small flowers are borne in summer, most commonly in an off-shade of red, but they may also be pink, blue, or yellowish. Variety 'Alba' has white flowers. Standard culture. Growth form amenable to pruning; can readily be kept to any size desired. Minimum temperature 40° F. Propagate by seeds or cuttings.

Syzygium jambos

See *Eugenia*

Tagetes erecta

See *Annuals*

Thunbergia

Family *Acanthaceae*. Evergreen vining plants with showy flowers. May be grown as container plants and will flower when 12 inches or so, but give their best in the ground or in large tubs. Standard culture.

T. alata (black-eyed-susan vine)   Native to tropical Africa. Grows to 10 feet. Perennial but usually treated as an annual, being more trouble than it is worth to overwinter. Not really a greenhouse plant (it is normally used outdoors for its summer flowers and quick growth), but a greenhouse permits an earlier, stronger start for the seeds in spring and a longer period of

bloom. Bears orange, yellow, or white flowers with a dark purple throat. Minimum temperature 50° F. Propagate by seeds.

T. grandiflora   Native to northern India. Grows to 20 feet. A magnificent twining vine for the greenhouse. Bears voluptuous blue flowers in fall, winter, and spring. Heart-shaped leaves are large and dense, casting heavy shade. Vigorous growth once it is well established. A breathtaking sight trained up the north wall of a greenhouse. Prune to keep in bounds, but otherwise it maintains good form. Minimum temperature 40° F, but well-established plants will recover from light frost. Propagate by seeds or cuttings.

Tibouchina

Family *Melastomataceae*. Native to tropical America. Evergreen shrubs, including one often grown in the greenhouse:

T. urvilleana (T. semidecandra) (glorybush) Native to tropical America. Grows to 16 feet. An exceptional container plant that

begins blooming when small, grows not too swiftly in a pot, and is amenable to pruning. After about five years the plant grows too large and can be replaced with cuttings already struck, which root readily and bloom quickly. The plant is indeed worth the effort, for its large deep blue flowers, carried for much of the year; its long, felted leaves, fuzzy to the touch as well as the eye; and its open, shapely, treelike growth. It may also be grown in the ground, in which case it soon proves itself more a vine than a shrub, and an exceedingly vigorous one at that. In the density of its growth it is very likely to be attacked by mealybugs. Standard culture. Prune for shapeliness. Frost-tender, though comfortable right down to 32° F. Propagate by cuttings, which should not be enclosed but left open to free circulation of air, with careful attention to keeping the medium moist.

Trachelospermum jasminoides

Zantedeschia aethiopica

Zantedeschia pink

Tillandsia cyanea

See *Bromeliads*

Trachelospermum

Family *Apocynaceae*. Species listed native to temperate Asia. Evergreen vines that form attractive, dense mats of small leaves on a supportive surface and bear fragrant white flowers in summer. Other genera can serve the same function of providing a close vertical covering, most notably *Ficus pumila* and *Hedera helix* (ivy), but *Trachelospermum* has the considerable advantages of restrained growth and significant flowers. Standard culture. Propagate by cuttings, which can be slow to establish. Prune to keep in bounds or, with continued tip pruning, to form a bush shape. Susceptible to mealybugs. Minimum temperature 40° F for best results, but hardy to 20° F.

T. asiaticum Grows to 15 feet. Leaves darker and less striking than *T. jasminoides* and flowers smaller, but the plant is somewhat hardier. Blooms April to June.

T. jasminoides (star-jasmine) Grows to 15 feet. New foliage is light green, maturing to a dark, lustrous tone. Blooms June to July.

Tropaeolum

See *Annuals*

Tulipa

See *Bulbs for Forcing*

Vallota speciosa

See *South African Bulbs*

Vanda

See *Orchids*

Viola

See *Annuals*

Vriesea hieroglyphica

See *Bromeliads*

Zantedeschia
Calla

Family *Araceae*. Native to tropical and temperate Africa. Stately plants with large, lance-shaped leaves. Large petal-like spathes surround the rigid yellow rod (spadix), made up of tiny flowers, which are actually petal-less. Very good container plants, providing bright splashes of color when in bloom and a distinctive foliage pattern at all times except during dormancy. Easily grown; standard culture. Plants revel in moist, even wet conditions when growing, then require a brief period of drying off and dormancy in summer. Minimum temperature 40° F. Propagate by division as dormancy ends in late summer or by seeds.

Z. aethiopica (Z. africana) (common calla) Leaves grow to 1½ feet, flower stems to 3 feet. White petallike spathes appear primarily in spring and summer. Needs less summer rest than other species but tolerates dryness then.

'Crowborough' is hardy to 12° F. This is of limited value,
however, because the leaves are killed by only light frost (the tuber endures) and do not appear again until the following fall, resulting in a very short period of growth.

'Devoniensis', 'Godfreyana', and 'Little Gem' are more free flowering and smaller than the unimproved form of the common calla.

Z. albomaculata (spotted calla) Leaves are spotted white and grow to 2 feet. Spathe is pale yellow to white with a reddish blotch at the base, spring to summer.

Z. elliotitana (golden calla) White spotted leaves grow to 10 inches long. Spathe matures from greenish yellow to golden.

Z. rehmannii (red calla) Grows to 1 foot. Pink spathe in May. Usually available as variety 'Superba', which has deeper pink spathe. Species has been hybridized with others to produce a very colorful range of cultivars.

Zinnia

See *Annuals*

DIRECTORY OF COMMON NAMES

The following plants, familiar to many gardeners by their common names, are listed in the "Plant Directory" under their scientific names.

African-lily *Agapanthus*
Amazon-lily *Eucharis grandiflora*
Angel-wing *Begonia coccinea*
Angel-wing jasmine *Jasminum nitidum*
Angel's-wings *Caladium* × *hortulanum* (see *Cactaceae*)
Australian fuchsia *Correa*
Baboonflower *Babiana*
Barbados-cherry *Malpighia glabra*
Barberton-daisy *Gerbera jamesonii*
Bird-of-paradise *Strelitzia reginae*
Bird's-nest fern *Asplenium nidus* (see Ferns)
Bishop's-cap *Astrophytum myriostigma* (see *Cactaceae*)
Black-eyed-susan vine *Thunbergia alata*
Blacktree *Aeonium arboreum* (see Succulents)
Bloodflower *Haemanthus katharinae*
Bluebush *Eucalyptus macrocarpa*
Blueginger *Dichorisandra thyrsiflora*
Blue-marguerite *Felicia amelloides*
Bonfire *Columnea* (see Gesneriads)
Boston fern *Nephrolepis exaltata* (see Ferns)
Bunny-ears *Opuntia microdasys* (see *Cactaceae*)
Butterfly orchid *Oncidium papilio* (see Orchids)
Cacti *Cactaceae*
Calla *Zantedeschia*
Cape-cowslip *Lachenalia aloides*
Cape-jasmine *Gardenia jasminoides*
Cape-primrose *Streptocarpus* hybrids (see Gesneriads)
Carnation *Dianthus caryophyllus* (see Annuals)
Carolina-jasmine *Gelsemium sempervirens*
Carrionplant *Stapelia* (see Succulents)

Chain cactus *Rhipsalis paradoxa* (see *Cactaceae*)
Chile-jasmine *Mandevilla laxa*
Christmas-pride *Ruellia macrantha*
Cider gum *Eucalyptus gunnii*
Cigarplant *Cuphea ignea*
Common gardenia *Gardenia jasminoides*
Common geranium *Pelargonium* × *hortorum*
Common heliotrope *Heliotropium arborescens*
Coral gum *Eucalyptus torquata*
Coralberry *Ardisia crispa*
Cow's-horn *Euphorbia grandicornis* (see Succulents)
Croton *Codiaeum*
Crown-of-thorns *Euphorbia milii*
Curryplant *Helichrysum italicum*
Daffodil *Narcissus* (see Bulbs for Forcing)
Dancing-ladies *Globba winitii*
Darling River pea *Swainsona galegifolia*
Desertrose *Adenium obesum* (see Succulents)
Donkey's-tail *Sedum morganianum* (see Succulents)
Easter cactus *Schlumbergera bridgesii* (see *Cactaceae*)
Everlasting *Helichrysum*
False-heather *Cuphea hyssopifolia*
Firecracker-plant *Crossandra infundibuliformis*
Flame-of-the-woods *Ixora coccinea*
Florist's coleus *Coleus blumei* var. *verschaffeltii*
Florist's cyclamen *Cyclamen persicum*
Florist's geranium *Pelargonium*
Flowering-maple *Abutilon*
German-violet *Exacum affine*
Giant toadplant *Stapelia gigantea* (see Succulents)
Glorybower *Clerodendron thomsoniae*
Glorybush *Tibouchina urvilleana*
Glory lily *Gloriosa rothschildiana*
Gloxinia *Sinningia speciosa* (see Gesneriads)
Golden gum *Eucalyptus eximia*
Golden trumpet vine *Allamanda cathartica*

Granadilla *Passiflora*
Grand-duchess oxalis *Oxalis purpurea*
Grapehyacinth *Muscari* (see Bulbs for Forcing)
Guava *Psidium guajava* or *Feijoa*
Guernsey-lily *Nerine sarniensis* (see South African Bulbs)
Gum tree *Eucalyptus*
Hare's-foot fern *Polypodium aureum* (see Ferns)
Hoop-petticoat daffodil *Narcissus bulbocodium*
Hyacinth *Hyacinthus* (see Bulbs for Forcing)
Iron-cross *Begonia masoniana*
Ivy geranium *Pelargonium peltatum*
Jadeplant *Crassula argentea* (see Succulents)
Java-glorybower *Clerodendrum speciosissimum*
Jellybeans *Sedum rubrotinctum* (see Succulents)
Jungle-geranium *Ixora javanica*
King protea *Protea cynaroides*
Kumquat *Fortunella* (see *Citrus* and *Fortunella*)
Ladder fern *Nephrolepis cordifolia* (see Ferns)
Lady's-slipper *Paphiopedilum* (see Orchids)
Leopardplant *Ligularia tussilaginea* 'Aureomaculata'
Licorice-plant *Helichrysum petiolatum*
Lily-of-the-Nile *Agapanthus*
Lipstick-plant *Aeschynanthus obconicus* (see Gesneriads)
Loquat *Eriobotrya japonica*
Magicflower *Achimenes* hybrids (see Gesneriads)
Malabar-plum *Syzygium jambos* (see *Eugenia*)
Mandarin orange *Citrus reticulata* (see *Citrus* and *Fortunella*)
Marigold *Tagetes erecta* (see Annuals)
Martha Washington geranium *Pelargonium* × *domesticum*
Mexican-bush sage *Salvia leucantha*
Meyer lemon *Citrus meyeri* (see *Citrus* and *Fortunella*)
Mickey-Mouse plant *Ochna serrulata*
Miniature holly *Malpighia coccigera*

Monkeyplant   *Ruellia makoyana*

Moth orchid   *Phalaenopsis*
(see Orchids)

Nasturtium   *Tropaeolum* species
(see Annuals)

Nightblooming cereus   *Selenicereus
grandiflorus* (see *Cactaceae*)

Old-lady cactus   *Mammillaria
hahniana* (see *Cactaceae*)

Pansy orchid   *Miltonia* (see Orchids)

Parachuteplant   *Ceropegia
sandersonii*

Passionflower   *Passiflora*

Pencilleaf   *Gasteria caespitosa*
(see Succulents)

Peppermint-stripe   *Oxalis versicolor*

Persian-shield   *Strobilanthes
dyeranus*

Persian-violet   *Cyclamen persicum*

Pineapple   *Ananas comosus* (see
Bromeliads)

Pineapple guava   *Feijoa sellowiana*

Pinkball dombeya   *Dombeya ×
cayeuxii*

Pink-powderpuff   *Calliandra
haematocephala*

Australian fuchsia, *Correa*

Pitanga   *Eugenia uniflora*

Poet's jasmine   *Jasminum officinale*

Pomegranate   *Punica granatum*

Ponderosa lemon   *Citrus medica ×
limon* (see *Citrus* and *Fortunella*)

Pot-marigold   *Calendula officinalis*
(see Annuals)

Pricklypear   *Opuntia ficus-indica*
(see Cactaceae)

Rabbit's-foot fern   *Davallia fejeensis*
(see Ferns)

Rainbow cactus   *Echinocereus
pectinatus* (see *Cactaceae*)

Rattail cactus   *Aporocactus
flagelliformis* (see *Cactaceae*)

Regal geranium   *Pelargonium ×
domesticum*

Rosaryvine   *Ceropegia woodii*

Roseapple   *Syzygium jambos*
(see *Eugenia*)

Rose-of-China   *Hibiscus rosa-
sinensis*

Rosemary   *Rosmarinus officinalis*

Sacred-flower-of-the-Incas   *Cantua
buxifolia*

Sage   *Salvia*

Sand-dollar   *Astrophytum asterias*
(see *Cactaceae*)

Scarboro-lily   *Vallota speciosa*
(see South African Bulbs)

Scarlet-plume   *Euphorbia fulgens*

Snapdragon   *Antirrhinum majus*
(see Annuals)

Snowdrop   *Galanthus* (see Bulbs
for Forcing)

Society-garlic   *Tulbaghia violacea*
(see South African Bulbs)

Spanish-shawl   *Heterocentron
elegans*

Stag's-horn fern   *Platycerium
bifurcatum* (see Ferns)

Starcluster   *Pentas lanceolata*

Star-jasmine   *Trachelospermum
jasminoides*

Stock   *Matthiola incana*
(see Annuals)

String-of-hearts   *Ceropegia woodii*

Surinam-cherry   *Eugenia uniflora*

Swan River daisy   *Brachycome
iberidifolia*

Sweetolive   *Osmanthus fragrans*

Sweet orange   *Citrus sinensis* (see
Citrus and *Fortunella*)

Sword fern   *Nephrolepis cordifolia*
(see Ferns)

Tangerine   *Citrus reticulata* (see
Citrus and *Fortunella*)

Tea-tree   *Leptospermum*

Thanksgiving cactus   *Schlumbergera
truncata* (see *Cactaceae*)

Tiger orchid   *Odontoglossum grande*
(see Orchids)

Tingiringi gum   *Eucalyptus
glaucescens*

Tulip   *Tulipa* (see Bulbs for Forcing)

Violet   *Viola* (see Annuals)

Wax-agave   *Echeveria agavoides*
(see Succulents)

Wildcoffee   *Mitriostigma axillare*

Winter daphne   *Daphne odora*

Yellowflax   *Reinwardtia indica*

Yesterday-today-and-tomorrow
Brunfelsia calycina

Zebra haworthia   *Haworthia fasciata*
(see Succulents)

Zebraplant   *Aphelandra squarrosa*

Zonal geranium   *Pelargonium ×
hortorum*

MAIL-ORDER SOURCES

The nurseries listed here provide plants or seeds by mail. The information on suppliers was correct at the time of publication. Write for a catalog or list before ordering.

Avon Bulbs
Upper Westwood
Bradford-on-Avon
Wiltshire BA15 2AT
England
Rare and choice bulbs; catalog $1

Botanical Society of South Africa
Kirstenbosch, Claremont 7735
Republic of South Africa
Seed list; membership $19

W. Atlee Burpee & Co.
Warminster, PA 18974
Seeds, bulbs, plants

Camellia Forest Nursery
125 Carolina Forest Rd.
Chapel Hill, NC 27514
Unusual camellias and other warm-temperate species; send 45¢ in stamps for catalog

Chiltern Seeds
Dept. HC
Bortree Stile
Ulverston, Cumbria LA12 7PB
England
Large selection of seeds

Cook's Geranium Nursery
712 N. Grand
Lyons, KS 67554
Pelargoniums; catalog $1

Cornelison Bromeliads
225 San Bernardino
N. Fort Myers, FL 33917
Bromeliads; send stamp for list

Peter B. Dow & Co.
Box 696
Gisborne
New Zealand
Unusually large selection of exotic seeds

Endangered Species
Box 1830
Tustin, CA 92680
House and greenhouse plants; three seasonal catalogs $5

Forestfarm
990 Tetherhoe
Williams, OR 97544
Unusual plants, including eucalyptus; catalog $2

Glasshouse Works
Box 97
Stewart, OH 45778-0097
Greenhouse plants

Gossler Farms Nursery
1200 Weaver Rd.
Springfield, OR 97478-9663
Warm-temperate species, primarily trees and shrubs

Hillier Nurseries Ltd.
Ampfield House
Ampfield, Romsey, Hants.
SO5 9PA
England
Wide range of unusual plants; catalog $1

K & L Cactus & Succulent Nursery
12712 Stockton Blvd.
Galt, CA 95632
Cacti and other succulents; catalog $2

Logee's Greenhouses
55 North St.
Danielson, CT 06239
Wide selection of greenhouse plants; catalog $3

Mellinger's
2382DC Range Rd.
North Lima, OH 44452
Plants

Montrose Nursery
Box 957
Hillsborough, NC 27278
Cyclamen species

Nindethana Seed Service
Narrikup
Western Australia 6326
Native seeds

Nuccio's Nurseries
3555 Chaney Trail
Altadena, CA 91001
Camellias and azaleas

Pacific Tree Farms
4301 Lynwood Dr.
Chula Vista, CA 92010
Greenhouse fruit plants; catalog $1.50

Park Seed Co.
Box 31
Greenwood, SC 29647
Seeds and bulbs

Parsley's Cape Seeds
1 Woodland Rd.
Somerset West 7130
Republic of South Africa
Native seeds

Plumeria People
Dept. Exotics
Box 820014
Houston, TX 77282-0014
Greenhouse plants; catalog $1

Potterton & Martin
Moortown Rd.
Nettleton, Caistor, Lincs.
LN7 6HX
England
Bulbs

Rainbow Gardens
1444 Taylor St.
Vista, CA 92084
Cacti and other succulents; catalog $2

Clyde Robin Seed Co.
Box 2855
Castro Valley, CA 94546
Seeds

Rust en Vrede Nursery
Box 231
Constantia 7848
Republic of South Africa
Native seeds

Singer's Growing Things
17806 Plummer St. H
Northridge, CA 91325
House and greenhouse plants; catalog $1.50

Siskiyou Nursery
2825 Cumming Road
Medford, OR 97501
Smaller and hardier greenhouse plants; catalog $2

Thompson & Morgan
Box 1308
Jackson, NJ 08527
Seeds

INSECTARIES

Pest-controlling insects can be mail-ordered from the following insectaries. Write for a catalog or list.

Beneficial Biosystems
1603-A 63rd St.
Emeryville, CA 94608

Plants of the Southwest
1812 Second St.
Santa Fe, NM 87501

Rincon-Vitova Insectaries, Inc.
Box 95
Oakview, CA 93022

INDEX

Note: Page numbers in italic type indicate references to illustrations. Most common names used in this book are listed on pages 106–7 and are therefore not included in this index.

U.S. *Measure and Metric Measure Conversion Chart*

		Formulas for Exact Measures			Rounded Measures for Quick Reference		
	Symbol	When you know:	Multiply by:	To find:			
Mass	oz	ounces	28.35	grams	1 oz		= 30 g
(Weight)	lb	pounds	0.45	kilograms	4 oz		= 115 g
	g	grams	0.035	ounces	8 oz		= 225 g
	kg	kilograms	2.2	pounds	16 oz	= 1 lb	= 450 g
					32 oz	= 2 lb	= 900 g
					36 oz		= 2¼ lb	= 1000g (1 kg)
Volume	pt	pints	0.47	liters	1 c	= 8 oz	= 250 ml
	qt	quarts	0.95	liters	2 c (1 pt)	= 16 oz	= 500 ml
	gal	gallons	3.785	liters	4 c (1 qt)	= 32 oz	= 1 liter
	ml	milliliters	0.034	fluid ounces	4 qt (1 gal)	= 128 oz	= 3¾ liter
Length	in.	inches	2.54	centimeters	⅜ in.		= 1 cm
	ft	feet	30.48	centimeters	1 in.		= 2.5 cm
	yd	yards	0.9144	meters	2 in.		= 5 cm
	mi	miles	1.609	kilometers	2½ in.		= 6.5 cm
	km	kilometers	0.621	miles	12 in. (1 ft)		= 30 cm
	m	meters	1.094	yards	1 yd		= 90 cm
	cm	centimeters	0.39	inches	100 ft		= 30 m
					1 mi		= 1.6 km
Temperature	°F	Fahrenheit	⅝ (after subtracting 32)	Celsius	32°F		= 0°C
	°C	Celsius	⅝ (then add 32)	Fahrenheit	212°F		= 100°C
Area	in.²	square inches	6.452	square centimeters	1 in.²		= 6.5 cm²
	ft²	square feet	929.0	square centimeters	1 ft²		= 930 cm²
	yd²	square yards	8361.0	square centimeters	1 yd²		= 8360 cm²
	a.	acres	0.4047	hectares	1 a.		= 4050 m²